WE THE RESILIENT

Wisdom for America
from Women
Born Before Suffrage

Edited by

Sarah Bunin Benor

and

Tom Fields-Meyer

Be inspired
from Tom's mom
Lora

LUMINARE PRESS

WWW.LUMINAREPRESS.COM

Printed in the United States of America

Cover Design: Claire Flint

Cover photos: top row: Miriam Nelson (right photo by Eduard Pastor); middle: Gladys Cornelius; bottom: Estelle Liebow Schultz

Luminare Press
438 Charnelton St. Suite 101
Eugene, OR 97401
www.luminarepress.com

LCCN: 2017935530
ISBN: 978-1-944733-19-3

For our wonderful children,
Aliza, Dalia, and Ariella Benor
and Ami, Ezra, and Noam Fields-Meyer.
We hope the wisdom of these women,
born three generations before you,
inspires you throughout your lives.

TABLE OF CONTENTS

You may encounter many defeats,
but you must not be defeated.
In fact, it may be necessary to encounter the defeats,
so you can know who you are,
what you can rise from,
how you can still come out of it.

— MAYA ANGELOU

FOREWORD

BY SENATOR BARBARA BOXER

As I recounted in my memoir, *The Art of Tough*, I first ran for office in 1972, the same year that Richard Nixon won the White House, defeating George McGovern in 49 of the 50 states.

Campaigning as a Democrat for the Marin County Board of Supervisors, I faced a steep uphill battle. I still remember knocking on the door of one woman who told me that if I was elected, I would be neglecting my four children. Never mind that I had only two!

I lost that election, and it didn't feel good. Two things helped me recover. One was reading an article by Gloria Steinem, who said women shouldn't take losses too personally—sometimes we're just a bit ahead of our time. The other was my son Doug, who woke up the next day and asked, "Mom, can you make me a peanut butter and jelly sandwich?"

What I learned is that life goes on, no matter how deep the disappointments. You pick yourself up, and you keep fighting. Because this is our country, and it's worth fighting for.

No one knows that better than the women whose voices make up this wonderful book. They have seen so much: the Great Depression, the Second World War, Vietnam, Watergate, and so much more. They have faced disappointment and loss. And yet they have all done what we women do: they have carried on with persistence and with dignity.

Like all of the women in this book, I supported my friend Hillary Clinton for president. I worked hard to get her elected, and I was heartbroken by her loss. But Hillary made history. As the first female nominee for a major party, she shattered that glass ceiling. She won the popular vote by millions. And she showed everybody the determination and strength of women.

Four years after I lost that election in Marin, I ran again. This time I won. And six years after that, I ran for Congress, and—against all odds—won that election, too. A decade later, I won a seat in the U.S. Senate.

The year I arrived in Washington, there were two women in the Senate. I never would have believed that 25 years later, in 2017, there would be 21 female senators.

As the remarkable women in this book remind us, progress comes, but it takes time and effort. You build on success, and you learn from your failures. I am confident that we will see the day when women are equally represented in Congress and we send a woman to the White House. In the meantime, I hope we can all learn what these women teach us: never stop working for what's right.

INTRODUCTION

BY TOM FIELDS-MEYER AND SARAH BUNIN BENOR

It started with a single photograph.

In early October of 2016, Sarah posted a picture on Facebook of her grandmother, Estelle Liebow Schultz. In the portrait, the bespectacled Grandma Estelle, who is 98 and lives in Rockville, Maryland, was flashing a radiant smile and holding up her mail-in ballot for November's presidential election. Sarah included a caption with her grandmother's words: "Estelle L. Schultz, who was born two years before women had the right to vote, marked her absentee ballot for the first female president, Hillary Clinton."

The post generated an immediate and overwhelming response, far beyond anything Sarah had experienced on social media. "This moved me to tears," wrote one friend—a reaction echoed by many others.

One of those commenters was Tom, an author and journalist, who suggested that there must be thousands of women like Estelle, born before the Nineteenth Amendment was adopted in 1920, who shared her enthusiasm for Clinton's candidacy. Perhaps it was worth finding a way to capture their stories.

Within days, the two of us joined forces—along with Sarah's mother, Roberta Benor, and Tom's wife, Shawn Fields-Meyer—to launch a website. We called it I Waited 96 Years!, and it celebrated these women and marked the historic moment we were eagerly anticipating.

We started small, wrangling a handful of friends to share photos of their grandmothers, along with quotes from the women explaining the significance to them of casting a ballot for Hillary Clinton. Then, with the help of social media and a significant boost from a BuzzFeed story, word spread quickly.

Within a week the website found a large audience, eventually attracting over 196,000 views and tens of thousands of follows and shares on Facebook and Twitter. Media organizations from as far as Australia, Japan, and Israel covered the story. Outlets from BBC News to Slate, from Cosmo to NPR ran the story. Even the comedian Samantha Bee took notice, splashing photos of the website's women as the backdrop during her election-eve monologue on her late-night show, *Full Frontal*.

Among the hundreds who shared the site on Facebook were entertainer Rosie O'Donnell and Wendy Davis, the Texas state senator who famously filibustered a restrictive abortion bill. Davis added this comment to her post: "Talk about heart-warming! #ImWithHer (and her and her...)."

Even the candidate herself took notice of the site, which eventually profiled 186 women between ages 96 and 105. Secretary Clinton mailed personal thank-you notes to Estelle and many of the other women who appeared on the site. "I read your marvelous profile on the website 'I Waited 96 Years,'" she wrote. "Thank you...for giving me such a wonderful dose of encouragement in these final weeks."

And then came Election Day.

To say the least, the results left much of the country shocked and dismayed. For many Americans, Hillary Clinton's defeat wasn't simply a loss at the polls, but a moment of crisis, a blow to their faith in the country's democratic institutions, its spirit of openness and inclusion.

Looking at the election's results, they saw an America they did not recognize. Given the electorate's sharp divide and the victory of a candidate so many saw as unqualified and too extreme, many had the same question: How can we go forward?

A few days after the election, two friends independently suggested a palliative idea: What if we pose that very question to the same group of extraordinary women who voiced such enthusiasm for electing a woman president? Where do we go from here? What can we learn from how the nation has weathered challenges in the past? And what's your best advice for facing the future?

Who better to answer these essential questions than these strong and durable women, who have witnessed a century of turbulent history and endured? Who better to offer the wisdom and perspective so desperately needed now?

Even before Election Day, when the women were sharing their life stories for the I Waited 96 Years! website, we had noticed a consistent theme emerging from their narratives: resilience. These women have lived through the Great Depression, World War II, the McCarthy era, the Cold War, the Civil Rights movement, Vietnam, and much more. Most have lost husbands; many have outlived multiple spouses. A large proportion have also lost children. They have coped with disease, unemployment, and dislocation; they have faced sexism, discrimination, and spouses and siblings heading off to war.

Yet they endure, many full of optimism and hope—even now. While they are seldom asked for their views publicly, these women have deep and timeless wisdom to share.

From a 100-year-old retired social worker from New Jersey: "I hope young people will come together and be activists to resist Trump and watch out that he doesn't get away with things. I also think it's very important for people to keep a sense of humor. It helps no matter how bad things get."

From a 96-year-old retired teacher from Missouri: "This country needs people to stand up and be heard, not through violence or rage, but through faith and struggle."

And from a 98-year-old from a small town in upstate New York: "No matter what happens, you must be tough, be strong, and go on. Be involved, be helpful, make a difference. You can't let your feelings of fear overwhelm you. You must deal with life as it happens. You can't be weak. You must fight for your rights."

This book had its roots in the excitement of a historic moment. That moment didn't transpire in the way many had hoped and dreamed it would. But disappointment is nothing new to these women. In their nine or ten decades of life, they have learned and grown from personal loss, communal crises, and national challenges. Our hope is that their wisdom, perspective, and grace can help the country—and all of us—follow the advice of Julia Cook, 101, from Pasadena, California: "Keep moving forward."

QUESTIONS AND ANSWERS

About *We the Resilient*

How were these women chosen?

All of the women appearing in this book were among the 186 who voluntarily submitted their photographs and statements to our pre-election website, iwaited96years.com. We sent follow-up questionnaires to 185 of the women (one had died after she mailed her absentee ballot, but before the election). Of those, 55 provided answers.

Why don't more of the women appear in the book?

Some women who had appeared on the website were not able to respond to these questions because of health problems. A few had died in the days or weeks following the election. And one granddaughter told us that her family simply didn't have the heart to tell her grandmother about the election results.

Why the separate section about the election?

The I Waited 96 Years! website generated a great deal of excitement and energy. We include a sampling of entries here in order to capture some of that spirit and to offer a sense of the women's enthusiasm and their compelling life stories. Also, it allowed us to feature women who did not submit their stories and advice for the Wisdom section.

How current are the women's ages, and why do some entries refer to Donald Trump as president-elect?

The ages listed are as of December 1, 2016. Participants submitted their responses in November and December 2016—before Trump's inauguration. The editors opted to preserve their phrasing.

Why did some women answer one or two questions, but others many more?

Each woman received the same questions with the option to answer as many as she chose.

Why do some entries include information about offspring, while others don't?

The participants had discretion to choose which personal information to highlight.

Did all of the women write their own answers?

Some of the women wrote their own responses, while in other cases family members or friends interviewed the subject and submitted the answers. We edited their words only lightly, for the sake of clarity and consistency.

Why aren't more women of color included?

We made great efforts to attract a diverse selection of women for the site, contacting various organizations that might help recruit participants. In the end, though, we were limited to those who chose to participate.

Who sponsored this project? Is it connected to a political party?

Both I Waited 96 Years! and *We the Resilient* are independent projects, not sponsored by or affiliated with any political campaign, candidate, or organization. However, the authors plan to donate a portion of the proceeds to the League of Women Voters, the Southern Poverty Law Center, and other charitable causes suggested by the women featured in the book.

Where does the book's title come from?
At the Women's March in January 2017, we saw several posters with the phrase "We the Resilient Have Been Here Before." The posters featured a Native American, fist in the air, protesting the Dakota Access Pipeline. Ernesto Yerena, the artist who created the poster, told us the image is a portrait of "Granny Helen Red Feather, a Lakota elder / activist who has been fighting for indigenous rights most of her life." Especially with this information, we decided that the phrase "We the Resilient" was perfect as the title for our book.

Poster for Women's March on Washington, January 2017, designed by Ernesto Yerena for the Amplifier Foundation's We the People campaign, in collaboration with photographer Ayşe Gürsöz; reprinted with permission from Ernesto Yerena

VOTERS

ANTICIPATING A HISTORIC MOMENT THAT NEVER ARRIVED
Voices from the *I Waited 96 Years!* Website

It was supposed to be the moment we broke through that final glass ceiling.

Millions of Americans were eagerly anticipating November 8, 2016, as the day when—after 240 years as a republic—we would elect a woman president.

That prospect was particularly sweet for a certain group of voters, women born before the Nineteenth Amendment guaranteed women the right to vote.

Sharing their eager anticipation, we launched our website, I Waited 96 Years! (iwaited96years.com), on October 20, less than three weeks before Election Day, welcoming women to share their photographs and tell us why this moment mattered.

The submissions started slowly, with one or two women each day writing to tell us of their excitement and hopes. As word spread, that trickle became a torrent. In the 48 hours before the polls closed, it seemed that a new submission arrived every few minutes.

In all, 186 women shared their stories. They ranged in age from 96 to 105 and came from 36 states and the District of Columbia. Two pairs of twins chimed in. The daughter of a slave. A retired Broadway choreographer.

Though all were enthusiastic about voting for Hillary Clinton, their reasons varied. Many were particularly focused on electing a woman. Others felt that she was simply the most qualified candidate, regardless of gender. Some were lifelong Democrats, active in progressive causes. Others voiced admiration for past Republican presidents but just thought it was Secretary Clinton's time.

A large portion of the voters were immigrants or the children of immigrants. Some still live in their towns of birth, while most have relocated at least a few times. The women had worked in a wide range of occupations, including nurse, real estate agent, chemist, seamstress, secretary, hair stylist, homemaker, teacher, salad chef, fashion model, puppeteer, and Coast Guard first mate.

And the top girls' names of the 1910s (according to the Social Security Administration) were well represented: eleven Marys, nine Helens, six Ruths, five Margarets, and four Dorothys.

Of course, that much-anticipated moment did not happen. Surely someday another woman will come along to shatter that glass ceiling. In the meantime, we share a sampling of some of our favorite submissions to I Waited 96 Years! in the hope that the energy and enthusiasm these women expressed in those exciting days will continue to inspire and offer hope for the future.

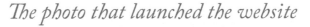

The photo that launched the website

ESTELLE LIEBOW SCHULTZ, 98

Rockville, Maryland

- Born June 1918 in New York City
- 2 children, 3 grandchildren, 4 great-grandchildren
- Retired educator, former assistant superintendent of the Compton Unified School District in California

"Recently, I was diagnosed with a serious heart condition and am now in home hospice. I am following this campaign carefully, and I decided that I would like to live long enough to see the election of our first woman president. When I was marking my absentee ballot for Hillary Clinton, it occurred to me that this wish is even more poignant, because I was born in 1918, two years before women achieved the right to vote. To see such an accomplishment in my lifetime is momentous. I encourage all of my fellow nonagenarians to follow me in marking your ballot with a sense of pride in a life long-lived and a country making history."

photo by Michelle Holley

ANNE WAINSCOTT, 99
Covington, Kentucky

- Born February 1917 in Cincinnati, Ohio
- Worked as fashion illustrator for 45 years, drawing work by designers such as Christian Dior and Elsa Schiaparelli from the '30s through the '70s
- Known for creating some of the best illustrations in the industry

"I determined that I was going to live long enough to vote for Hillary Clinton for president. At 99 and almost nine months, I am thrilled to say that I accomplished my goal. I was born of two immigrant parents who came to this county with nothing but their intelligence and work ethic. My parents and others like them helped build this country. My generation defeated Hitler, and I had relatives in Europe murdered by the Nazis. I will not see what we have built be destroyed by racism and fear of immigrants. America is too good for that, and I know that the first woman president will preserve what generations before her helped build. Hillary 2016!"

REGINA FOLEY, 96
Millbrae, California

- Born July 1920 in Germany (naturalized citizen)
- Grew up in Germany, where she saw the catastrophic effects of fascism
- Married U.S. Air Force serviceman from New York City who was serving in Germany
- Moved to his various stations until 1968, when they settled in California

"After 96 years, I'm helping make history by voting for not just the most qualified candidate, but for the first woman POTUS! My husband was the son of Irish immigrants and a lifelong FDR New Deal Democrat who worked with the Civilian Conservation Corps during the Depression. He passed away in 2007. We didn't always agree on politics, but I know if he were still alive he would be thrilled to cast his ballot with me to elect Hillary as our next president."

MARGARET JOHNSTON, 99
Santa Rosa, California

* Born July 1917 in Minneapolis
* Graduated from the University of Minnesota
* Served as Navy lieutenant during World War II
* Was one of the two original female vice presidents of the Pacific Stock Exchange
* Twin children, 4 grandchildren, 7 great-grandchildren

"Of course I am voting for Hillary. I *will* live to see the day a woman becomes president."

Editors' note: Margaret Johnston died on November 19, just 11 days after the election. Her granddaughter shared this remembrance:

"I have tons of stories of her—including how she challenged her boss for equal pay/benefits back in the late '50s when she worked for the Pacific Stock Exchange. She was also in the Navy during World War II and worked for the Office of Censorship. Single mom (widowed when her twins were age ten) that worked her tail off to make the world a better place. She was devastated with the news of Trump's victory. Although she was 99, her death was a surprise, as she had been in great spirits/healthy."

GLADY BURRILL, 97
Honolulu, Hawaii

* Born November 1918 in Vancouver, Washington
* Licensed pilot
* Farmer, Christian, and compassionate friend
* Holds Guinness World Record as oldest woman to complete a marathon (age 92, Honolulu Marathon)
* 6 children, 19 grandchildren, 32 great-grandchildren

"This election is about hope, optimism, respect, and qualifications. Hillary has them all. From one strong woman to another."

VERNICE WARFIELD, 101
Rochester, New York

- Born February 1915 in Texarkana, Texas
- Her father—born a slave—and mother educated her and ten siblings
- Became a Methodist minister in the 1940s, pastoring at the AME church in Auburn, New York—previously Harriet Tubman's church
- Married Robert Warfield, brother of the singer William Warfield
- Volunteered in schools teaching remedial reading, writing, and mathematics
- Pioneered integrated PTAs in her city and programs for interracial adoptions in the '70s
- Worked as a civil rights leader and community organizer for the Red Cross, Urban League, NAACP, Church Women United, and other groups
- 3 children, 7 grandchildren, 13 great-grandchildren, 4 great-great-grandchildren

"I didn't want an absentee ballot, even though I will be 102 in a couple of months. I wanted to make my way to my polling place, where I've been going for over sixty years, to cast my vote in person on this historic day. In my 101 years I've experienced and seen so much! I'm confident all Americans will do what's right and bring a woman to the top. I've got my 'power-pantsuit' on in honor of Hillary Clinton. Women know what to do and how to do it!"

ALYSE LAEMMLE, 100

Hermosa Beach, California

- Born May 1916 in Chicago
- Retired life-insurance agent who earned a place on Mass Mutual's "million-dollar roundtable"
- Was married 57 years
- 2 daughters, 5 grandchildren, 4 great-grandchildren

"I think Hillary Clinton is an outstanding human being. I am not voting for her because she is a woman, but because she is an outstanding human being."

PRIMETTA GIACOPINI, 100

San Jose, California

- Born June 1916 in Torrington, Connecticut
- Taken in by an older, childless couple after her mother died when she was two
- In 1929 they retired to Italy, taking her along
- Italian authorities ordered her back to U.S. in 1940 because she was American
- Traveled in convoy through Vichy France and Franco's Spain to Lisbon, then crossed Atlantic on small ship packed with refugees
- Returning to Torrington, got work with General Motors and met husband, Bert, carpooling
- Quit job to care for daughter with spina bifida (who went on to Harvard)
- Retired to San Jose and still lives independently at home

"It's about time we got a woman in there! The men have had plenty of time and have just screwed things up."

LUISA CECI JACOBSON, 96
Queens, New York

- Born May 1920 in Vallecorsa, Italy
- Was the first women from her town to attend college
- Started at the University of Rome, but had to stop because of World War II
- After the war, attended the University of Southern California, then New York's Hunter College
- Speaks English, Spanish, and Italian fluently
- Taught language in New York City and Long Island schools
- 4 children, 6 grandchildren, "and many grand-pets"

"I was born three months before women had the right to vote. I broke my own glass ceiling by being the first woman from my hometown to attend university. Women have made progress in this world, that's for sure. It's not a man's world anymore; it's becoming a woman's world. Never in my whole life did I think I would live to see this day. We need a woman president for our country, and it's going to be Hillary Clinton!"

KATHLEEN DUFFY, 97
Broomall, Pennsylvania

- Born August 1919 in Philadelphia
- Served as Democratic committeewoman in Delaware County, Pennsylvania
- Never missed voting in person in primary or general election
- Walks four miles daily

"In all my years, I have never missed voting on Election Day. I so look forward to this one!!! Having a woman as president of the United States means that a young girl will know that she can grow up to be anything she dreams. I was very active as a Democratic committeewoman for years, working alongside other women, but always helping to elect a man. It is very rewarding now to know that a woman will soon hold the highest position in our land. Election Day cannot get here soon enough!"

MAE GRACE LANGE, 96
Cordova, Alaska

- Born May 1920 in Katalla, a village in the territory of Alaska that no longer exists, to Tlingit Indian and Danish parents
- Knows how to live off the land and make a home out of very little
- Operated a commercial fishing vessel for more than 50 years
- 6 children (1 deceased), and dozens of grandchildren and great-grandchildren

"You know, I was born before women were allowed to vote, and now I get to vote for a woman for president."

FRANCES LEHMAN, 97
Wilmette, Illinois

- Born September 1919 in Chicago
- Was the only woman in her MBA class at New York University in 1941
- Longtime community volunteer and activist
- 3 children, 8 grandchildren, 6 great-grandchildren

"I cast my first ballot for Franklin D. Roosevelt in 1940, and in every presidential election since, I've voted for the Democrat. I was proud to vote early for Hillary Clinton, and I'm scared of Donald Trump. In the summer of 1935, I went to Germany with my family. I've thought a lot about that trip this year. After he made the arrangements at the U.S. consulate in Stuttgart, my father brought his sister Frieda, her children, and several more distant cousins to America. I want my grandchildren and great-grandchildren to live in a country where everyone gets treated equally, where we all care for one another, and where we welcome people from all over the world."

CONSUELO LOPEZ, 96
San Antonio, Texas

* Born November 1919 in Austin, Texas
* 2 children, 8 grandchildren, 15 great-grandchildren

"When I was born women had no voice and were not allowed to vote. Now we are about to make history and have a woman president for the United States. I never thought in a million years I would see that happen. It's a glorious time."

photo by Mike Belleme

NORA LOURIE GUND PERCIVAL, 102
Boone, North Carolina

* Born October 1914 in Samara, Russia
* Survived the Russian Revolution and emigrated to New York City at age eight
* Graduated from Barnard College in 1936
* Worked as an editor and manager at American Management Association
* Served as Barnard's alumni director, editing the alumni magazine in retirement
* Started a local newspaper in Kent, Connecticut, with husband
* Published first of three memoirs at age 87
* Has participated in local writers' group for more than two decades and still edits for friends
* 5 children, 11 grandchildren, 7 great-grandchildren

"I have stood for and worked for the strength and wisdom of women most of my life. It is time to let a woman lead this country. As a survivor of the Russian Revolution I know a bit about the fragility of rights and freedom. I cherish what we have in this country—vote for Hillary!"

ECHO GARVIN RIDER, 97
Miller Ridge, Oklahoma

- Born October 1919 in Miller Ridge, Oklahoma
- Born, raised, and still lives on father's Cherokee Indian allotment and homestead
- Taught school starting at age 20, for total of 41 years
- During World War II was recruited to paint airplanes and, later, ships
- Taught every grade (1st through 12th) and served as principal
- Active in civic organizations promoting her community, heritage, and history
- Raised cattle and raced quarter horses

"I am proud to be an American, and I am voting for Hillary Clinton to be our nation's first female president."

"AUNTIE LOU" LOUISE RUCKER, 99
Redwood City, California

- Born January 1917 in San Francisco, California
- Parents were immigrants from Guadalajara and Chihuahua, Mexico
- Now lives surrounded by wonderful family and friends
- Proudly voted early for Hillary Clinton

"I believe that Hillary has a steady, fair mind and she will be a terrific leader. I would like a woman running the country. Also, Trump can kiss my a--. Wait a second, on second thought, I don't want him near my a--."

SYLVIA SCHULMAN, 99

Oceanside, New York

- Graduated high school at age 16
- Taught elementary school for more than three decades
- 4 grandchildren, 3 great-grandchildren

photo by Alison Schulman

"This vote is not just because Hillary is woman, nor because I am a Democrat. It's to show that we as women can do anything we want, especially when we have worked hard in our careers to obtain the experience necessary to excel. It's nice to show my granddaughter and great-granddaughter that the sky is the limit and they can do anything a man can do. I'm proud to say that I'm with her."

MADELINE ROSENBERG, 101

Hartsdale, New York

- Born July 1915 in Brooklyn, New York, to Russian immigrants
- Had three brothers who fought in World War II
- Lived in California and New York City
- Worked as a fashion model in New York City
- Ran upstate New York retail business with her husband
- 2 children, 4 grandchildren, 4 great-grandchildren

"It is exciting to vote in this election. Women are getting where they belong!"

photo by Nanette Soffen

B.RUTH KERMAN SOFFEN, 102
South Orange, New Jersey

- Born April 1914 in Brooklyn, New York
- Bootlegged with her family during Prohibition to help pay off debt
- Hitchhiked to Florida in her 20s
- Worked as a civilian secretary for the U.S. government during World War II and won a 50-dollar office pool for guessing when Japan would surrender after taking dictation on the atom bomb
- Won an arbitration with the New York City Unemployment Office without a lawyer after being wrongfully denied benefits in 1957
- As secretary/bookkeeper in the furniture business with her husband in Union City, New Jersey, was among the first to extend credit to Cuban immigrants
- Enjoys writing poems for family and friends' birthdays and special occasions, reading, crocheting, and playing bridge
- 1 daughter, son-in-law, 3 grandchildren, 1 great-grandchild

"Thrilled when Dr. Oz presented her with a cake on her 100th birthday, B.Ruth revealed, 'You have to have something exciting to look forward to every day; that's what makes the heart beat.' When the village president of the Township of South Orange presented her with an official proclamation recognizing her 102nd birthday, B.Ruth couldn't stop exclaiming, 'The Lady Mayor!!!' Now, she is excited to be able to cast her vote for the most competent candidate in years and a long-awaited first female president of the United States!"

SORA FRANKEL, 96
Parkland, Florida

- Born November 1919 in Brooklyn, New York
- Earned a bachelor's from Brooklyn College and a master's in teaching from Hofstra University
- Taught 28 years (elementary school, special-needs children, and college), including one year in Indonesia
- Hosted more than 100 overseas visitors through various exchange programs
- Was married for 70 years
- 2 children, 4 grandchildren, 7 great-grandchildren

"Peace and quiet! I can really and actually vote for a woman. Not only am I voting, but I can vote for a candidate who is a woman. She was an outstanding person from a very early age. She was Number One all the way along. She is not just an ordinary woman, but a woman with many gifts. To me, this is not just a woman—this is a very special woman."

RACHEL KOTIKE, 98
Santa Ynez, California

- Born February 1918 in Bronx, New York
- Worked side-by-side with husband in his New York pharmacy
- Was active in Democratic Party, American Jewish Congress, and Hadassah
- Still keeps up with politics daily
- 1 daughter, 4 grandchildren, 1 great-grandchild

"After a lifetime of being politically involved, I feel I contributed to the reality of a woman becoming president. I am grateful that at 98 years of age I am witnessing this historic event in our country."

ELEANOR SOKOLOFF, 102
Philadelphia, Pennsylvania

- Born June 1914 in Cleveland, Ohio
- Studied piano at Cleveland Institute of Music and then Curtis Institute of Music
- Still on the faculty at Curtis, where she has taught piano for 80 years
- Has taught more than 75 students who have gone on to perform with the Philadelphia Orchestra

"I was born six years before women had the right to vote, so this election means so much to me. I have supported Hillary Clinton since her husband's first run for the presidency and said I would vote for her for president at that time. Now, I get to do exactly that!"

LUNG HSIN WU, 98
Portland, Oregon

- Born February 1918 in Beijing, China
- Came to the U.S. in 1941 to attend Stanford; never returned because of the Chinese Revolution
- Worked at SRI International until 1997 retirement
- Moved to Portland in 1997 with her son

"My vote means another step toward equity for women! I voted for Hillary eight years ago, and I'm still alive to vote again. This time she'll win!"

MARGARET THOMPSON, 100
Stockton, California

- Born September 1916 in Portland, Oregon
- Graduated from Oregon State University
- Taught high school
- Community leadership roles in PTA, League of Women Voters, and hospital auxiliaries
- Received 100th birthday wishes from President and Mrs. Obama
- Married 58 years
- 4 children, 10 grandchildren, 10 great-grandchildren

"I first voted in 1940 for FDR, and I have voted the Democratic ticket ever since. I am voting for Hillary Clinton because she has years of experience. She has been pushing for women's rights and really the rights of everyone, and because of that I think we can trust her. I am voting for her because I want the world to go forward, not back."

Editors' note:
Margaret Ann Thompson died on November 10, 2016, surrounded by loved ones. Her family remembered her as a loving woman with a sharp mind, deep faith, and strong commitment to "the liberal ideals that have made the United States a beacon of openness."

Though her retirement community's guidelines forbade political signage, she proudly posted signs on her screen door: OBAMA, PROUD DEMOCRAT, and READY FOR HILLARY. A granddaughter once asked her how to handle a relative with opposing political views. "Speak up," Margaret told her. "Otherwise, people won't know what you believe."

After following the presidential campaign closely, Margaret asked her daughter Pam the morning of Election Day, "Are they dancing in the streets? Are they singing because she won?" Convinced Hillary Clinton would win, Pam assured her they were indeed. Before the day was over, Margaret went into a deep sleep. She died two days later. "Heaven has gained a truly great lady," a Catholic priest and longtime friend said later. "I only feel sorry for one person, St. Peter, since he's the one who will have to break the news to her."

WISDOM

Wisdom and Perspective for a Challenging Time

"How can we move forward from here?"

That was the question many of us were asking ourselves in the days just after the November 2016 presidential election. We felt shocked, disoriented, and disillusioned. Many of us simply didn't know what to do with ourselves.

When you face challenges or disappointments, the best advice often comes from people who have traveled down that road before. So we sought the wisdom of the women of I Waited 96 Years! Born before 1920, they had lived through some of the nation's most challenging times. *Surely,* we thought, *they would have insight for this moment.*

We got back in touch with the participants and posed questions in six categories:

When in your life have you experienced personal disappointment, tragedy, or unexpected loss? How were you able to overcome those setbacks?

What's the most helpful advice you ever received about recovering from difficult times?

You have lived through many periods that were challenging for our nation: the Great Depression, World War II, the McCarthy Era, the struggle for civil rights, Vietnam, and many others. Please recall a time when the national outlook seemed bleak, and tell us what was key to our recovery and resilience.

When in your lifetime was this country at its best?

What have your experiences been with sexism, and how have you persevered? What advice do you have for girls and younger women?

What other wisdom do you have for our country at this moment—particularly for young people who feel disappointed, disillusioned, or in despair?

One of the first women to reply shared her memory of the day of President Kennedy was assassinated. Few could imagine how the country could recover, she said. But it did.

That insight, simple yet profound, provided some measure of comfort. And that was just the beginning. As you'll see on the following pages, the 55 women who responded shared decades upon decades of experience: personal losses, financial setbacks, national calamities, family tragedies. Mostly they shared their collective resilience, the human capacity to rebound from even the most challenging circumstances.

These women haven't solved the problems facing our country, but together they offer a collective vision of how each of us can face the future.

RUTH ALBERTS, 98
Stroudsburg, Pennsylvania

- Born April 1918 in Roemerville, Pennsylvania
- 3 children, 10 grandchildren, 15 grandchildren, "and a dynamite smile!"

When the country was at its best
Right after the election of Roosevelt we were stalled at a crossroads. Yet what changed things for the country was the faith we had in him as our leader. He stabilized the country. We need more of this—the feeling of being united, not divided.

Advice for the country at this moment
What we have to do now is think more clearly and seriously about what's needed in this country. Do not sit by; take action.

Ruth as a child (top), at age 17 (left), and at 27

INEZ ALCORN, 96
St. Maries, Idaho

- Born May 1920 in El Paso, Texas
- 3 daughters, 5 grandchildren, 9 great-grandchildren, and a set of great-great-grand-twins

How the country recovered from challenging times

The first time I ever heard a voice on the radio, it was Al Smith, who ran against Hoover. The people next door had a crystal set. My parents were probably as unhappy with the election of Hoover as I am with Trump. Al Smith wasn't elected because he was a Catholic and the people in the southeast hill country of Oklahoma were sure that the Pope would come to rule the U.S.

My parents always took a newspaper if one was available. They were sharecroppers in Oklahoma, and when we left the farm, it was in a covered wagon. For two years we just traveled from one small sawmill to another. Those of us in the South didn't notice the Depression as much as the rest of the country did. We were poor before and poor after. We ate squirrels and rabbits and fish, and my mother built her own furniture. She was often ill, and I started making biscuits at age seven, standing on a box. But my parents always tried to keep my sister and me in school. My main goal in life became to see that my own children had an education.

My experiences with sexism and advice to young women

When I went to work in 1956 as a checker in a large chain grocery store, I was paid 15 cents an hour less than a 16-year-old box boy. I made 85 cents, and he made a dollar. That did not change until we joined a union.

Advice for the country at this moment

The key to a good life is to find work that you like and have an aptitude for. Have a couple of hobbies that you enjoy. The challenges people face are many, but life is meant to be enjoyed as much as possible, to find joy in small things.

Photo of Inez by Cathy Britschgi

"Life is meant to be enjoyed as much as possible."

"This country has managed to avoid a dictator, a police state, or a government based on arbitrary decisions."

GLADYS ELLEN ATKINS, 96
Trenton, Missouri

- Born May 1920 in Humansville, Missouri
- Taught high school English and reading starting at age 18
- After retiring at age 72, delivered Meals on Wheels to other seniors
- Played church organ and piano for 75 years
- Reads voraciously and loves learning
- 5 children, 8 grandchildren, 9 great-grandchildren

How I have overcome personal setbacks

I experienced the loss of my husband when he was only 47, and I was faced with raising our five children. I also experienced the tragedy of the death of two of those children. I have withstood my personal tragedies by perseverance and belief. I have relied on family, and they have been a help when I needed them. My faith in a greater goodness that unites us after death—and that death is just another journey—are part of the belief that helps me.

The best advice I ever got about recovering from difficult times

The best advice I received was from two of my college professors, who both became friends of mine. Their advice was not spoken, but rather was their unspoken assumption that I would not give up—that I would continue to stand strong and fight my way forward through the obstacles put before me by man and by chance. I also received support from my rural community, particularly the school I taught in and the church where I played organ.

How the country recovered from challenging times

Looking back in history, recent or more distant, this country has overcome challenging problems. There have been times when this nation has committed unjustifiable acts, but it has endured—particularly because this nation is comprised of diverse, multi-ethnic groups that are almost all immigrants. They built a nation based on a strong, yet flexible, document that is respected and not rejected by new leaders coming into power.

The seesaw of power between two parties and the fight for balance between them also seems to have moderated how extreme our nation gets before change occurs. This country has managed to avoid a dictator, a police state, or a government based on arbitrary decisions, rather than laws that are administered with the goal of equality.

When the country was at its best

This country has not been its best yet. Equality for all ethnicities, genders, faiths, and lifestyles is still an ongoing struggle, and until these goals are realized, this country must continue to strive to get to the best that it can be. I hope to live to see that time.

My experiences with sexism and advice to young women

My advice for girls and younger women is to push yourselves to be the best possible person you can be. Embrace family and friends, but make sure you work toward your goals, using your will, your strengths, and your choices. Do not let family, friends, or society tell you what you can or cannot achieve or what you should or should not be. And this is true on personal, spiritual, and career fronts.

Advice for the country at this moment

This country needs people to stand up and be heard, not through violence or rage, but through faith and struggle. This country is the way it is today because of the sharing, discussing, and implementation of ideas by all races, nationalities, and creeds.

But one of the most important things is knowledge. We live in a time of unprecedented ability to obtain information on the most complex or simplest things, but people have to understand and use that knowledge. They have to separate truth from opinion. They have to work to educate themselves, not just let others tell them what to believe.

Fight to learn and grow and listen to others to see if they can help you to learn or grow. Read, listen, learn, and think for yourself. Read fiction, nonfiction, news, history, classics, cartoons, and fairy tales. Expand your minds and never quit learning new or old things.

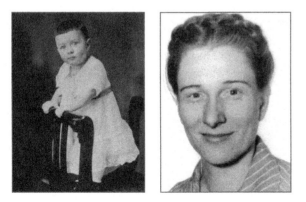

Gladys in 1922 (left) and in the late 1930s

"We deserved a woman president."

DOROTHY BARTON, 98
Davenport, Iowa

- Born March 1918 in Lyons, Michigan
- After high school, worked for a doctor for three dollars a week plus room and board
- Later worked for a coal company for six dollars a week
- After borrowing 100 dollars from grandmother to attend nursing school, worked as a nurse for two doctors
- Returned to college to earn BA in Behavioral Science
- Still lives independently, preparing her own meals, reading, emailing friends and family, and playing Words with Friends
- Was married for 63 years
- 2 daughters, 5 grandchildren, 10 great-grandchildren

How I have overcome personal setbacks
It was April 1929. The Wall Street crash was about six months away. But our family was having its own crash. Dad had lost his job. All the money we had was his last paycheck. We quickly decided to leave Oregon and return to Lyon, Michigan. Getting there needed to be cheap and include few possessions. With help from my mother's brothers, we bought a used Buick Touring car, vintage 1918, for 75 dollars. It needed a little tuning. On May 7, we headed east, back seat loaded.

Those three thousand miles challenged our old Buick, and repairs depleted our funds. By wire, Grandma sent money twice. We reached Iowa, where we suffered cold weather. In Joliet, Illinois, we went to bed at 4 p.m. to get warm. It was still dark and very early when we had breakfast—on me. We had to get gas for the last leg to Michigan. I had offered money before, with no takers. This time my parents took it. I had sold my doll buggy back in Oregon, and the money I earned was the last cash we had.

Late in the afternoon, I saw a sign that read, "Homemade Pies. Lyon's Restaurant." We soon rolled under the trees at Grandma's house. The old Buick stopped. Later it was sold for ten dollars to a farmer who hauled it away. We were home safe.

The best advice I ever got about recovering from difficult times

Grandma never lectured; she was an example. She didn't know she was teaching, and I didn't know I was being taught. These life lessons I observed, but only later was able to list: Do your best at a job. Don't complain. Squirrel away a little money. Be dependable. Get an education. Stand by your family. Be patient. She made sure her two sons attended school, and when I needed 100 dollars to attend nursing school, she provided it.

As a preteen, she had taken care of a girl named Libby Minkler, who lived on a farm in northern Illinois. Libby had lost both of her arms above the elbow in a farm accident. Libby's mother knew that my grandmother had only a second-grade education and urged her to attend third grade when she accompanied Libby to school. Libby was also an example of perseverance. She learned to write and paint with pens in her teeth. We still have one of her paintings.

Grandma was frugal. The minimum electric bill one could pay the Lyons Power Company was one dollar. Grandma made sure she never went over that amount. She used the non-electric Bissel sweeper daily and the electric sweeper once a week. Lights were off unless

Dorothy's grandmother, Matilda Willitt (top); Dorothy as a registered nurse in 1941 (bottom)

*"Do your best at a job.
Don't complain.
Squirrel away a little money.
Be dependable.
Get an education.
Stand by your family.
Be patient."*

someone was in the room. She once ordered me to, "buy a quart of raspberries, but only at or below 14 cents." She taught me to buy flour in 50-pound bags, bank the fire at night, and use the waste water to water the garden or bushes.

She took in boarders to supplement her husband's salary as a clerk at the local hardware store. I saw nine people eating at a table with a white linen tablecloth and napkins. I saw twelve white sheets being washed by hand and hung on the line and loaves of bread rising on the worktable. Grandma was in her sixties. Each night she cleared a path to the door in case she was summoned by the doctor to assist in a newborn's delivery.

How the country recovered from challenging times

Our country has been through many difficult times. Memorable for me were the Great Depression and World War II. I was a young mother during World War II. We had to make do, and we did. We tightened our belts and became creative and determined in overcoming adversity. We conserved and felt strong, knowing that our sacrifices were necessary for our freedom. We guarded our allotments, worked in factories, and enlisted in the military to help defeat tyrants. We remembered the wisdom and strength of our mothers and grandmothers.

Women have taught each other since this land was first settled, growing stronger with every adversity. We deserved a woman president.

Advice for the country at this moment

Hang out with like-minded people who are positive and forward-looking. Get an education. Get involved.

"My favorite time period was when Franklin Roosevelt was president."

EVELYN "GIGI" BERGMAN, 100
Detroit, Michigan

- Born October 1916
- 2 children, 5 grandchildren, 4 great-grandchildren

Evelyn (bottom left) at age two with her brother and sister (left); Evelyn as a high school senior

When the country was at its best

My favorite time period was when Franklin Roosevelt was president. The times were good financially. I had a job selling cosmetics at Sam's Department store in Bay City, Michigan, where my first daughter, Arlene, was born. I earned 20 dollars a month and had my own apartment. I had a lot of friends and we went out to eat at restaurants. I enjoyed my job and I got to take home free lipstick samples. There were a lot of women who worked with me and it was a good time in my life.

MIRIAM BERGMAN, 96
Pinehurst, North Carolina

- Born January 1920 in Copenhagen, Denmark
- Immigrated as a young child with her parents, Danish film stars
- Became a child star on New York's Yiddish stage
- Was married for 70 years
- 4 children, 5 grandchildren

Miriam as a girl and as an adult

How I have overcome personal setbacks

I pulled myself together and told myself, "I'm going to beat this. I'm going to overcome this." And eventually good came to me and it turned out all right.

How the country recovered from challenging times

During the Depression people who overcame it had to be determined to succeed and not despair.

When the country was at its best

I think FDR was the greatest president of all time. He was charismatic. He inspired everyone to emulate his high standards, inspired us to overcome and to use our best talents. I think when a president is doing a great job, there shouldn't be term limits.

My experiences with sexism and advice to young women

I would tell them to persevere, be the best you can be, and extend and stretch yourself.

Advice for the country at this moment

Dream the biggest dreams of what you want and then go for it, work for it, attack it as if your life depends on it. Everyone has disappointments. Life doesn't hand you a platter of all good. You have to take the good with the bad. Rejoice in the good. Take the bad and try to make it better.

"Take the bad and try to make it better."

33

"Instead of despairing, do something."

JULIET RELIS BERNSTEIN, 103
Chatham, Massachusetts

- Born July 1913 near Ferndale, New York
- Remembers accompanying her mother in a horse-drawn carriage to the polls in the first election in which women had the right to vote
- Encouraged by her mother, earned bachelor's degree from Brooklyn College
- Taught home economics in New York public schools
- Lifelong peace activist who for years coordinated Cape Cod chapter of Fellowship of Reconciliation, an international peace and justice group
- Served as president of local League of Women Voters chapter
- Inveterate follower of the news and writer of letters to the editor
- Awarded Boston Post Cane in February 2016 as Chatham's oldest resident

How I have overcome personal setbacks
When I was 14, my father committed suicide. When I was 42 my husband was suspended from teaching mathematics without pay, to be reinstated three years later. I was 61 when my youngest son was "kicked out of college" for neglecting his studies because of political activities, to return at 26 to another college from which he received his degree. When I was 80 my husband died from cardiac arrest while we

Juliet with her two sisters, 1920; in 2016, (above) when Juliet was awarded the Boston Post Cane for being the oldest person in Chatham, Massachusetts (photo by Robin Litwin)

Juliet at Glacier National Park, 1937

were walking on Thanksgiving Day, awaiting the arrival of our older son.

I was able to overcome all of these setbacks because of strength, resilience, and courage. I think I received these from my mother, who came from Russia at age 12 with her father, worked in a factory to help bring the rest of the family here, and was able to overcome my father's suicide through her strength, resilience, and courage. With no formal education, she inspired all four children to go to college.

The best advice I ever got about recovering from difficult times

I cannot recall having received any helpful advice from anyone. I always made my own decisions. As children growing up we knew what was right or wrong from our parents' behavior and attitudes, and mostly from my mother, since my father had died so young. During my marriage, my husband and I discussed everything before we made a decision about anything. I always received support from him in whatever I did. After my husband's sudden death I received support from family and friends.

How the country recovered from challenging times

The McCarthy Era was a difficult time for us. My husband was suspended through this, I was on maternity leave with a baby and we had no income. However, my husband was able to borrow from the pension system, do private tutoring, and was employed by a private school, and I returned to work.

I think the fact that my husband and I were able to discuss everything and became closer in our relationship were keys to my recovery and resilience. There were never any recriminations; I think I was always a strong, positive individual. And perhaps, too, I had "common sense," it was said.

The Great Depression was not too difficult for me because we lived in a farm-boarding house and always had a roof over our heads and plenty of food. I decided to return to school for a master's degree because work in my chosen field at the time was not available. The key was always strength and courage.

When the country was at its best

I think during the Roosevelt Era, after the country had gone through the Great Depression. There was hope. So many opportunities were given to people through the National Recovery Act. Schools and other places were built. The infrastructure was developed. The arts were encouraged. Different projects were initiated: the school lunch program, the Civilian Conservation Corps, the National Youth Administration, national parks and forests were developed, plays were performed, murals were painted in schools and postal buildings, homes were built. There was a caring attitude for people and country.

Another good time was the Kennedy and Johnson era, when civil rights and voting rights were enacted. We should know that government is needed to help improve the lives of all people, especially the most vulnerable; that needed services should not be provided by charitable or religious organizations; that is the role of government.

My experiences with sexism and advice to young women

Growing up, I never heard the word sexism. In the one-room schoolhouse and the small rural high school I attended, I never saw any difference in the ways boys and girls were treated, except that in high school there was no female gym teacher. The teacher was the basketball coach for boys, and in our so-called gym class he would throw us the ball and tell us to play.

There was this difference: most of the boys

Juliet with Ellen and Robert, 1943

were headed to college, whereas girls were not. They would take the secretarial course, rather than the academic course, which most of the boys took.

I really encountered sexism after I received my graduate degree. I was sent for a job interview. When I was about to sign the contract, I was told that if I got married, I would lose my job. I thought to myself, even though I had no boyfriend, that no one was going to tell me whether or not I could get married.

Of course there was sexism generally then, because girls were limited in the kind of career they could pursue—teaching, nursing, secretarial work, or marriage. Had I had the opportunities young women have today, I think I might have been a physician. That never entered my mind then.

Girls and young women have a world of opportunities. They can follow their dreams. But they must also be realistic. They have to see what their aptitudes are. They also have to consider whether or not they want to get married—because that may interfere with their career—and whether to have children.

Juliet with Ellen and Robert, 1947

When I got married you just assumed you would have children, and most women who married had no choice because contraception was not legal or easily available. I think young women take this all for granted, but with the new administration in this country now, everything that women have fought for may be lost. I think they should get involved with organizations that protect all of these rights that have taken decades to obtain.

Advice for the country at this moment

This is a very sad time in the history of our country. We must not, however, give up hope. I too am truly disappointed that we still do not have a woman president. We are supposed to be an example for the rest of the world, and here we are, not only unable to elect a woman, but we have elected a man with an ego who wants all power, a man who has hatred for all people except himself, whose administration will do damage to our country for years to come.

Instead of despairing, they must do something. Join an organization that can make changes. Engage in nonviolent protests. Write letters to the editor of your newspaper. Work with others who are like minded. Remember, as Margaret Mead said, "Never doubt that a small group of thoughtful, committed citizens can change the world. Indeed, it is the only thing that ever has."

Work to see that women will no longer be considered objects. Work to see that all people are treated with dignity, that all people have equal rights, for a peaceful world with the elimination of nuclear weapons. Be kind to all people with whom you come in contact. If you hear or see anything demeaning, don't be afraid to speak up. Laugh a lot; it is good for the soul and for your heart and lungs.

Believe me, I, too, at age 103, am disappointed not to see a woman president in my lifetime. They said when the Fourteenth and Fifteenth Amendments were passed that it was not women's time. It is long overdue. You, the younger generations, must bring it to happen.

CORNELIA "NEAL" COXE BREWSTER, 97

Carol Stream, Illinois

- Born April 1919 in Buffalo, New York
- Twin of Alice "Lal" Keith
- Happily married for 74 years
- Lifelong Democrat whose husband generally voted Republican
- 5 children, 11 grandchildren, 10 great-grandchildren

How I have overcome personal setbacks

My biggest personal disappointment was when my love, John Brewster, left me in September 1940 with the remark, "This relationship has no future." I turned to other boyfriends, but it was never the same. I tried to forget him, but I couldn't.

In February 1942, after fifteen months, he waltzed back into my life. He called me at the office, but he ran out of nickels and dimes so we did not decide on how to meet. I was 21 and had been having drinks with friends from work. When I arrived home at my parents' house, he was there. I suspected that he might show up, but I did not want my heart broken again. He said that he had seen a movie with Carole Lombard and started thinking about me with tears in his eyes. We sat in the parlor and played cards, and he took me to the movies the next day.

After a few months, he asked me to marry him, but I made him wait for a week before giving him an answer. Now, after 74 years, 5 kids, 11 grandchildren, and 10 great-grandchildren, I am so glad it all worked out.

"I didn't let my male colleagues get away with sexist remarks. Sometimes I even swore at them."

Cornelia on her wedding day

Best advice about recovering from difficult times

My boss at the British Purchasing Commission during the war, when my husband was about to be commissioned for World War II: "Just keep on trying; don't give up." It is good that I have always been an optimist.

How the country recovered from challenging times

The Great Depression was the hardest time for our family. Our lives were totally disrupted. My father lost his job at Archer Daniels and had to take another where he was collecting rents. We lost my favorite house and had to move to a much smaller house in a neighboring town. My twin sister and I had to change schools from Dwight School for Girls in Englewood to the public high school. (Actually, I liked the public school because there were boys there!)

The key to our recovery was first the programs of the FDR administration. I got a job with the National Youth Administration, which was like the WPA (Works Progress Administration), but for youth. That earned me money for clothes and a little entertainment (dancing to records). The longer-term recovery was from the war effort, which brought us all together.

When the country was at its best

At the end of World War II. We were all building houses and having babies. My husband got a good job as an actuary at the Prudential in Newark, New Jersey, and we bought our first house.

My experiences with sexism and advice to young women

We simply accepted a lot of the discrimination, including lower wages for women. We didn't know any differently because it had always been like that. We thought it was reasonable because men were supporting their families. However, I didn't let my male colleagues get away with sexist remarks. Sometimes I even swore at them. I also did not like the double standard that allowed men to fool around, but not women.

Advice for the country at this moment

I know we have to accept adversity as we have done in the past. I hope young people will face this situation with courage and stand up for what is right.

MARY BRUNO, 101
Tampa, Florida

- Born September 1915 in Italy
- 1 son, 2 grandchildren

The best advice I ever got about recovering from difficult times

I came to this country as a teenage girl, not speaking the language. Adjusting to a new home and learning English were very difficult. I was ready to enter teaching college before we came here, but was sent back in school because I didn't speak English. The teachers in Orange, Massachusetts, would spend their break time working with me, my sister, and my brother, helping us to practice and learn. They were very encouraging. In particular, Miss Edwards helped me a lot and always advised me to practice and never give up. That advice has stayed with me for my whole life.

When the country was at its best

After the war, when my husband returned from the service, everybody was happy. Things were starting fresh, the economy was good, every-

Mary Bruno with husband, Edmund, son, Edmund, and dog, Frodo

one believed the future was bright. People approached the future with a great deal of optimism. We could learn from that.

Advice for the country at this moment

My advice to young women is to always be yourself; be kind, and always try to be helpful to one another.

"Be kind, and always try to be helpful to one another."

"Turn off your TV occasionally and read a good book."

FAYE BUTLER, 98
Decatur, Georgia

- Born June 1918 in Council Bluffs, Iowa
- Taught in a one-room schoolhouse
- Married her college sweetheart, Bob
- 2 sons and 1 daughter

How I have overcome personal setbacks

The greatest tragedy in my life—as well as my family's—was the death of my brother during the Second World War. First Lt. Robert Samuel Evans, Army Corps of Engineers, was serving in Merrill's Marauders in Burma. When that terrible telegram arrived at my parents' front door in Council Bluffs, my sister Edith was an army nurse serving in the Pacific and my brother Bill, Coast Guard Reserve, was keeping the troop trains running out of Portland for the Union Pacific. I was teaching school in Anthon, Iowa.

My wonderful superintendent arranged for my substitutes and put me on the first bus out of Sioux City. We cried for two days, and our neighbors came with food and sympathy. They assured me they would look after my parents. The Clinkenbeards sat every evening with my parents for a month.

My father went back to his six-day work week, twelve-hour days. My mother went back to housekeeping, victory gardening, knitting socks for soldiers, and selling war bonds. I went back to teaching, folding bandages, and collecting scrap metal.

Two months later my husband, Bob, came home safe after nine months of patrolling for submarines over the Bay of Biscay. He had a

41

two-week leave and was slated for more flight training so he could be sent to the South Pacific. When I joined him in Pensacola, I took Red Cross nurses' training so I could volunteer in the local hospital.

That is where Bob and I were on V-J Day. Naturally, we joined the throngs of people in the streets, who were joined arm-in-arm, marching down the streets, cheering and singing. At that very time, my sister, Edith, back from caring for wounded soldiers in the Pacific, was confined to a troop ship docked off Seattle. She was back in the states on leave and due to be sent back. As Edith put it, "We had just helped to win the war, and they wouldn't let us off the ship to celebrate." Maybe it was just as well, because I read in the paper that four people were accidentally killed in the streets during the celebration.

Many months later my brother Bob's body was transferred to the national cemetery in Hawaii. His grave has been visited by my mother, brother, my son Sam, and, just recently, my sister's grandson.

Advice for the country at this moment

Work hard in high school and community college (if you cannot afford tuition at private colleges), so that you can make a living doing something you enjoy.

Eat well-balanced meals and exercise. If you don't have a sport or exercise program, take a brisk walk. Turn off your TV occasionally and read a good book. Learn how to do something with your hands besides tweeting and texting, such as cooking, sewing, knitting, quilting, gardening, woodworking, model building, or

Faye (top) reading to her oldest son, Sam; on her wedding day, wearing a dress and headpiece she made

even small household repairs.

If you simply must use your computer to communicate, use it to promote civility in our already great country. Cultivate good friends and be a good friend.

"I rarely remember to say World War II, to distinguish it from other wars, because it was so all-consuming."

PAULINE BUTTON, 96
La Verne, California

- Born May 1920 in Oakland, California
- Taught sixth grade for many years
- Also taught high school English; elementary school math, music, and piano; and adult-education sewing
- Happily married for 73 years
- 3 children and 5 grandchildren

How I have overcome personal setbacks

The most disappointing thing? Gosh, that is hard to pin down. It is so much easier for me to think of the exciting and fun things that happened in my life!

How the country recovered from challenging times

The war was challenging. I rarely remember to say World War II, to distinguish it from other wars, because it was so all consuming for four years of our lives. It directed every action and reaction. It was long, frightening, lonesome, terrible, and tragic. It changed our thinking, our habits, and perspectives. And it certainly clarified basic priorities.

Pauline (left) with her husband, Orville Button; with her second daughter, Diane Stillinger; above: photo by Catherine Hall Studios

Pauline as a young woman

My soon-to-be husband was sent to Kentucky for training. The first chance I got to visit, I went, not knowing how hard it would be to get there. With space prioritized for service members, I got bumped off an airplane, then a train, delayed, and ate stale sandwiches along the way. But I kept plugging along and eventually made it to Kentucky in time to get married before he went overseas.

After he left, I didn't know what to do at first. It was tough not knowing what to do, but I learned to be resourceful. I found I could help by rolling bandages for the troops, and by sending letters and pictures to keep morale up. You just use what you can use and figure it out; look for what is available to you. The more you get used to that, the easier it gets and opens up access through other angles. Think to yourself, "I think I can do it."

When the country was at its best

The '50s were such a wonderful time. After the war, people were happy and starting their families. From my point of view, it was the most satisfying, happy, and absolutely hands-down favorite period in my life.

"We've still got the best government in the world. Calm down and take it easy."

GERTA CAMPEN, 99
Durham, North Carolina

- Born November 1917, Wilmington, North Carolina
- Loves animals, Pink Floyd, and the feel of riding a motorcycle
- 3 children

Gerta, 1960s

Advice for the country at this moment

Think about your free country. Think about how you don't have to have loudspeakers all over the place telling you what to do, who's watching over you. I think people have forgotten what some of these other countries have gone through.

Take part in what's going on. We should at least know what's going on, and not just get all riled up when something happens that rubs us the wrong way.

I don't think Trump can get away with being a dictator. We've got too many safeguards. We've still got the best government in the world. Calm down and take it easy.

"I remember the morning Pearl Harbor was bombed. It was a sad and scary time for everyone."

SARAH PUILANI YOUNG CHING, 100

Keaau, Hawaii

- Born August 1916 in Honolulu, Hawaii
- Worked during World War II as an Army secretary
- Later worked as a preschool teacher, short-order cook, and salad chef
- 3 children, 4 grandchildren, 5 great-grandchildren

How I have overcome personal setbacks

In 1967 I was divorced with three children in high school. With the divorce settlement, I bought a little house near the beach and a '67 Mustang. I enjoyed working as a short-order cook, then became a salad chef at the Moana Hotel. When I retired, I went to culinary school and studied cake decorating.

The best advice I ever got about recovering from difficult times

My advice to my children was, "If there's a will, there's a way." Just a saying I've always remembered from my school days at the priory.

How the country recovered from challenging times

I remember the morning Pearl Harbor was bombed. Planes were above us, and I remember the *ratatatat* of gunfire. We were about to leave for church, and we rushed back to the house. We later were instructed to paint our windows black. I remember some of my Japanese friends were taken away, and I never saw them again. It was a sad and scary time for everyone.

When the country was at its best

In 1980, I retired at age 64. I took classes at the University of Hawaii. I was the oldest and the top of my class. I then joined several senior-citizen clubs. My favorites were tai chi, Scrabble, making feather leis, and ceramics. I later devoted my spare time to visiting my grandchildren. My friends and family knew to call early, because by 5:30 every morning I was out the door. Every day was an adventure for me.

My experiences with sexism and advice to young women

I went to Saint Andrews Priory, an all-girls school, and we learned that we could achieve whatever we wanted if we focused on our goals and worked hard. My father was a vegetable farmer; my mother took in ironing and made Hawaiian quilts. I had five sisters and two brothers, and later a baby brother. We were all encouraged to do well.

Advice for the country at this moment

Never ever give up. You can accomplish the impossible if you try.

HARRIET TERRY ROBINSON COHEN, 98

Margaretville, New York

- Born November 1918 in New York City
- Taught first grade and university
- Worked as agricultural field organizer for Catholic Charities
- Headed local hospital auxiliary and currently serves on its wellness committee
- Served on New York governor's Community Services Block Grant Advisory Council
- Honored as "citizen of the year" by hospital and "outstanding citizen" by county Office of the Aging
- 2 children, 4 grandchildren, 9 great-grandchildren

How I have overcome personal setbacks

The worst tragedy of my life was the loss of my son, Danny, from a sudden heart attack. I think of him every day. A loss like that—you never get over it. That's life: it happened, it's part of you, you must live with it.

What I try to do is think, "I am grateful I had him for 60 years. He was a wonderful person in my life."

"You can't let your feelings of fear overwhelm you. You must deal with life as it happens."

Although I choose to live in a nursing home, I still stay active. You can't sit and cry. I make a difference for my town; I am on the hospital auxiliary and help run the membership drive.

The best advice I ever got about recovering from difficult times

The best advice was from my mother. She lost a child—a baby—and she had a divorce. Yet with all she had to deal with, she always had a goal of helping others.

I remember anti-Semitic remarks written on the sidewalk near our home. It was a frightening time. I was in high school and Hitler was rising on the scene. It was the rise of fascism in Europe. My mother, although

Harriet (top) as American Red Cross Club Director, Saipan, 1945; at a rally for veterans' benefits, Albany, New York, 1947

spent her money to sponsor getting family and friends out of Europe. We welcomed them in our home in the Bronx. There was always someone staying with us. That greatly affected me.

How the country recovered from challenging times

I joined the Red Cross in World War II and was stationed in Saipan, in the Pacific. I had to take a train across the United States and then a ship from San Francisco. It was overwhelming and frightening. I had never been away from home before! And it was what there was to do. We each had to do our part. Those are the great moments of your life you will remember with pride.

Advice for the country at this moment

My mother taught me the importance of education. We were expected to go to college—three girls! We could live at home with her only if we stayed in school. I got my master's, my sister her PhD.

As a first-grade teacher, my joy was to take a person and teach them to read. After that, you have the world of knowledge available to you. I encourage every young child, girl or boy, get the best education you can, study, learn history, get the facts, and be courageous. No matter what happens, you must be tough, be strong, and go on. Be involved, be helpful, make a difference. You can't let your feelings of fear overwhelm you. You must deal with life as it happens. You can't be weak. You must fight for your rights.

not formally educated, read the paper, and we listened to the news. She worked tirelessly to build a business, supporting us, and she also

JULIA M. COOK, 101
Pasadena, California

- Born September 1915 in Cynthia, Kentucky
- Married until she was widowed in 1976
- 2 children, 3 grandchildren, 4 great-grandchildren

How I have overcome personal setbacks

I have had a wonderful life, but my greatest loss was that of my son, a police officer who was killed in the line of duty, protecting his fellow officers. There are no words to explain that loss other than "life-changing." I survived by keeping myself busy, working, and spending time with loved ones and friends. I still weep when I think about him and what the world lost when my son was killed.

The best advice I ever got about recovering from difficult times

Be stubborn, get up and go, and do the best you can with the support of family and friends. Be brave and find support wherever you can: friends, family, church, whatever.

How the country recovered from challenging times

Americans are strong and resilient people. They have a lot of stamina and support each other.

In the Great Depression, my father was a farmer in Kentucky, and we raised vegetables and farm animals. We raised tobacco for extra money. It was a tough go of it. Most people in my community were very generous with food. In the part of the country I lived in, we had rations, but no one went hungry and everyone came together.

During World War II, people worked with a purpose to support our troops. When our minds are focused on a common goal, we can do anything.

I worked a variety jobs during the war, while my husband was fighting in the Pacific theater. I worked in an ammunition factory, mail room, the Naval supply depot, repairing boat engines, and anything that needed to be done. Everyone worked together to support each other. We had to live with rations, like coffee, food, and butter. It was difficult, but we did without to support our country.

During Vietnam, I worked in a school cafeteria, and I saw the sadness and pain of the children

"Everyone was so happy that the war was over, and the soldiers were so grateful for everyone's support and sacrifice."

Julia in high school

whose parents were sent away and, worse, died. I did the best I could to help comfort them and make sure everyone had at least one meal during the day.

When the country was at its best

Our country was at its best at the end of World War II. The parades and joy were amazing. People were so happy, and everyone was out singing and dancing. We waited for the ships to come in and had gatherings and ate. When my husband's ship docked, I remember waiting and then seeing him as he came off. It was so wonderful. Everyone was so happy that the war was over, and the soldiers were so grateful for everyone's support and sacrifice.

My experiences with sexism and advice to young women

They think they have everything, but they don't. There is more to life than stuff. From what I see, so many young women don't have a sense of what is important, like family, friends, and community support. Women today have the opportunity for everything, but many don't even know what they need. Be true to yourself. Honor yourself. Keep your family and friends close because you will always need them. Also, don't take anything for granted or expect the world to hand you things. Work for everything you get.

I retired at the age of 84 after working in a school cafeteria for 34 years. At times I would babysit for a dollar an hour at night for wealthy people in Miami Beach. I never asked for anything I did not earn.

Advice for the country at this moment

Keep moving forward and remember that bad times come and they go. Family gets you through the rough times. But the key is education. I want young people to have the educational opportunities I worked so hard for my family to have. Education is the key.

My mother started her life off as an indentured servant, until she married my father. My father taught my mother to read and write by oil lamp. He taught her to count money so she could go to the store. My father imparted the importance of education on me, my siblings, and my mother. Because of the example he set for me, I was the first person to graduate from high school in my family. I was the valedictorian and class president of a class of ten in our entire county, and one of only two girls.

"I participated in marches for equal opportunities. The civil rights movement helped change life for the better."

GLADYS CORNELIUS, 99
Atlanta, Georgia

- Born June 1917 in Davisboro, Georgia
- 8 children, 21 grandchildren, 15 great-grandchildren
- Is a member of the "Young at Heart Club"
- Has been a faithful churchgoer
- Recently started piano lessons

How I have overcome personal setbacks

I remember as young girl going into a closet and praying. That helped me overcome whatever bothered me.

The best advice I ever got about recovering from difficult times

I never shared my problems with anyone. I kept them to myself and prayed to God for guidance.

How the country recovered from challenging times

I do not remember the Great Depression affecting my life. We were not rich, but life as I remember it was not bad. I never went hungry.

Gladys and her husband on Auburn Avenue, known as "Black Wall Street," 1939

Living in the South, there was a civil rights struggle. I participated in some of the marches

for equal opportunities. The movement helped change life for the better.

When the country was at its best
In the 1960s the economy was better and everyone got along. There was peace and love.

My experiences with sexism and advice to young women
During my earlier life, women stayed home, cooked, and cleaned. I also worked. Working allowed me to not be dependent on anyone. I would tell girls and younger women to get educated. Never stop learning, and join organizations that will strengthen you and keep you involved.

Advice for the country at this moment
When you feel life getting you down, think about something good. Do not let worry take place. Know there will be better days ahead.

Gladys with Elks Gate City Marching Unit #43 in 1970 (top); in 1949 at Paramount Studio, Auburn Avenue, Atlanta

53

"Always remember your right and civic duty to vote."

VERONICA (RONNIE) FLEMING DALE, 96
San Diego, California

- Born July 1920 in Sacramento, California
- Her father survived the 1906 San Francisco earthquake
- Frequently danced with girlfriends at San Francisco's Mark Hopkins Hotel during World War II
- Worked as a hair stylist and waitress
- Member of the Garden Club, Daughters of the Nile, and St. Francis of Assisi
- 5 children, 2 grandchildren, 2 great-grandchildren
- Survived breast cancer

How I have overcome personal setbacks
In my early twenties I lost my father to cancer. When I was 35, my husband passed in a tragic car accident, when I was six weeks pregnant and had four other children at home under age ten, one of whom was mentally challenged.

At 38, I found myself pregnant out of wedlock, which was looked down on. I made the difficult decision to give the baby up for adoption in the hopes he'd have a better life. When I was 41, my mother passed from diabetes. I was 44 when my only sibling (my brother) passed of a heart attack.

I have been married more than once because, in my day, a "lady" did not shack up,

Veronica at First Communion and at high school graduation, 1940

Veronica volunteering for Women's Ambulance Corp (left); with her mother, Lillian Fleming (top right); in 1969 (bottom right)

she got married. It's just the way it was—it was what society expected of you. I have outlived all of my mates. My most recent husband passed of cancer when I was 88. I was able to move through all the loss due to the values instilled in me by my parents, in the context of hard work and my faith in God.

My experiences with sexism and advice to young women

The advice I have for young women is to always remember you are a lady! Allow a man to be a man, let him open your door and pull out your chair. Always take care of yourself. Do what you want in life. Don't ever let anyone tell you, you can't do something. And always remember your right and civic duty to vote!

"Young people have no alternative but to take the initiative to maintain equity and equality."

EDITH DUNFEE, 102
New York City

- Born January 1914 in Staten Island, New York
- Married at 19 to delivery-truck driver
- Did not graduate from high school, opting instead for secretarial school
- Always worked, relying on extended family for childcare
- Created middle-class life in New Jersey, sending her children to college
- 2 daughters, 3 grandchildren, 5 great-grandchildren

How the country recovered from challenging times

The bad times were in the 1930s, when one's income was mostly so dreadfully low that many people, including us, seriously did not have enough money with which to buy food.

The good times came when we were introduced to labor unions. My husband was lucky enough to be able to join one.

When the country was at its best

The country was at its best, in my opinion, after World War II. Employment was high and there existed a wonderful, hard-working middle class.

Edith as a child with her siblings, Walter and Emily (twins), and their mother, Emily Drake

Edith (top left) with her daughters, Ethelyne (left) and Edith Ann (right), early 1940s; Edith as a young woman (top right) and at work, New York City, 1967 (bottom right)

The United States was a happy, prosperous place at that time. As for my husband and me, after World War II we never had the feeling that the country seemed bleak. Our goal was to work. We found comfort and joy in working for a good life for ourselves and our family. We were fortunate in that we had the union to help us do just that.

Advice for the country at this moment

With the recent election outcome and the current mood of the country, I certainly am fearful and concerned about our precious freedoms.

These are the freedoms for which my generation worked so hard. Freedom is freedom. There is no substitute. The young people of our country have no alternative but to stand up and take the initiative in order to maintain the goodness and generosity of heart that has kept this nation the best place on earth and to see that equity and equality keep their place in our society. This takes a great deal of effort. Our generation assumed that responsibility, and now it is up to the younger generation to carry the torch.

GERALDINE "JERRY" EMMETT, 102
Prescott, Arizona

- Born July 1914 in Rippey, Iowa
- Arizona resident since 1919
- Graduate of Arizona State Teachers College (now Northern Arizona University)
- Lifelong active Democrat

How I have overcome personal setbacks
When my husband went to war, when I lost my 69-year-old son, when I lost a baby girl and my only brother. I overcame those setbacks because I realize that happens to all human beings and because of my close relationship with God.

The best advice I ever got about recovering from difficult times
My parents told me that everyone faces difficulties; it's just part of life. My mother, Winnie, always said, "Stay close with God."

How the country recovered from challenging times
The Great Depression helped us to realize how we depend on each other for strength. What I

Geraldine at high school graduation, 1932

remember most about the Great Depression was that people cared and helped each other.

When the country was at its best
The response of America to the tragedy of Pearl Harbor, because the country was one. Pull together. Stand behind the country.

My experiences with sexism and advice to young women
Sexism seemed to disappear when women got the right to vote and they took over many men's jobs in World War II. Follow your dream.

Advice for the country at this moment
Stay there and keep trying. Be strong. Things will change. The only constant in the world is change.

"The only constant in the world is change."

DOROTHY FISCHER, 96
Rothbury, Michigan

- Born June 1920 in New Era, Michigan
- Was married 57 years
- Worked as secretary and then partnered with husband on family farm
- Raised registered Guernsey cattle, asparagus, nursery stock, and Christmas trees
- Served as township treasurer for four years
- Active in many community organizations
- 3 children, 2 grandchildren, 2 great-grandchildren

How I have overcome personal setbacks
I was devastated when my mother died when I was 14 years old. I loved her dearly. I was in tenth grade and staying in town during the week to attend school. I thought that I would have to drop out to take care of the family, but my father said, "No, education is too important." He said if we all worked together we could manage.

I was able to find a ride with a classmate who drove a car. I had to walk one and a half miles to meet him. I got up when my father went to do chores, made a fire in the cook stove, and made a big pot of oatmeal. Then I would wake my sister and she would take over. We did the washing in two tubs and scrub boards with a hand wringer between and the cleaning, etc., over the weekend.

There was no electricity. We even cooked dinner for the threshing crew. Neighbors often commented on how capable we were, and we were proud of it.

Later, my mother's widowed cousin and her eight-year-old son came to live with us. We knew her well and liked her. It was a good arrangement for all concerned, but I resented her. I didn't like being replaced. However, life was a lot easier for me, and I was finally won over. She proved to be a good stepmother and, incidentally, lived to be 98..

"I made less than a man with the same job. It seemed unfair, but I didn't say anything—I didn't want to get fired."

The best advice I ever got about recovering from difficult times

When I was a young teenager at Trinity Lutheran Church, Rev. Paulsen's sermon was on anger, and he included the quote, "Let not the sun go down upon your wrath." That seemed like good advice. I've tried to follow that all of my life.

How the country recovered from challenging times

I feel blessed to have been born an American. My parents purchased their first automobile in 1921, so I started life in the horse-and-buggy days. The early '20s were good times, but when the stock market crashed everything changed. Banks closed their doors. My two younger siblings and I had saved a total of 57 dollars, and we lost it all. My father later got a small portion of it back in scrip. Money was scarce, but we lived on a farm, so there was always food on the table.

In 1933 my mother thought my sister and I should have new Easter dresses. She searched the Sears Roebuck catalog and was able to buy us lovely voile dresses for under one dollar for both.

I was married on November 22, 1941. We went to Niagara Falls for our honeymoon, but we could not go on the Canadian side because Canada had already entered World War II. We returned late Sunday night and went straight to bed. When we awoke Pearl Harbor had been bombed; we were at war.

Franklin Roosevelt was a good president. He was a father figure and kept us calm with his fireside chats over the radio.

Dorothy as a baby
"in the horse-and-buggy days"

A presidential couple everybody loved was the Kennedys. They were young, vibrant, and stylish. Jackie made the pillbox hat famous, and Jack didn't wear a hat at all. Soon American men were tossing theirs aside. My 22nd wedding anniversary was a very sad day for America and the world—John F. Kennedy was assassinated.

My experiences with sexism and advice to young women

I got my first job shortly after graduating from high school and worked until my first son was born. I loved my work and was paid well for the times. When my boss got discharged because he wanted a raise in his pay, I was offered the position. I was given a small increase, but not as much as he had been earning. It seemed unfair, but I didn't say anything; that's the way it was, and I didn't want to get fired.

"Throughout my life there was an unacknowledged belief that men were somehow superior."

MARY ELLEN SWITZER FITTS, 98

Chelsea, Michigan

- Born January 1918 in Knoxville, Tennessee
- Born the 5th of 10 children to a strong woman influenced by the women's suffrage movement in her hometown of Ithaca, New York
- Taught school before marrying and raising 4 children in Ohio and Michigan
- After her husband died unexpectedly in 1965, returned to work in social services and continuing education
- 3 surviving daughters, 6 grandchildren

How I have overcome personal setbacks

My worst experiences were the death of my husband in 1965, from a sudden heart attack when he was only 52, and 15 years later, when my only son drowned in a kayak accident at just 34.

Two things helped me most through those losses. First, I had four children who were still dependent on me. Having my children, taking care of them, watching them, and listening to them was such a big part of my life.

I think I just coped day to day. I also had the help of some dear friends, who just showed up and did things and helped at moments when I felt I couldn't do anything. I've always been so grateful for that.

Also, I've felt like the deep love we had in my marriage never ended.

The best advice I ever got about recovering from difficult times

I don't recall any advice directly. But I was very influenced by witnessing the Depression and its effects on my parents in the 1930s. My father died of untreated cancer in 1939, with no pension benefits, even though he had a good job. My mother had to sell our home.

Several of the children were old enough to work. Unlike the older children, the youngest were not able to go to college, because Mother couldn't afford to pay their tuition. Tuition then was a mere pittance compared to today. Still, she couldn't pay it. So the youngest girl went to secretarial school, and the boy was drafted at 18 into the Army. After the war, he went to college on the GI Bill. My older brothers and one sister, a WAC (member of the Women's Army Corps), were also in the war.

No matter what, my mother was just calm, strong, and non-complaining. She had dependents; her youngest child was mentally handicapped, and she had to take care of him. She was very strong. I had just told her I was pregnant the same day she died of a stroke. I was always glad she knew I was going to have more children; she had loved having lots of children (ten!).

When the country was at its best

I think it was the actions that President Roosevelt took to get the country out of the Depression, his Pubic Works Administration, and other items that he passed to give people jobs with a living wage. And then the start of World War II—I think there was optimism that we would win that war.

The other best thing in my lifetime was the election of President Obama. I thought that was just tremendous for the country to elect a black president. And for the legislation he was able to pass, like health care—that's very important—and because of his eloquence in speaking to the citizens.

My experiences with sexism and advice to young women

Any problems I had, I don't remember thinking of them happening because I was a woman. In general, throughout my life, there was an unacknowledged belief that men were somehow superior, stronger; they were the ones who had the money. But I can't think of any

Mary at age 5, 1923
(photo by John Albert Switzer)

Mary with her first two children, 1947
(photo by Paul M. Fitts, Jr.)

time that I was directly disadvantaged by the action of men.

I had jobs in continuing education and as a social worker. At two of those jobs I had women for bosses, and they encouraged me. One of them was an Eleanor Roosevelt–kind of wife to a successful professor.

My other job was to get faculty members to write distance-education courses. I had conflict with my boss, a younger man. He and his boss were secretive and made me feel I was very "stupid and wrong," but I kept a record of things he did or didn't do, and I would go to the human relations department and talk with them about it. So fortunately for me they had a record, because when the university was downsizing, my boss tried to fire me, but because I had this record he was not allowed to fire me. To young women of today:

1. Acknowledge that men are stronger than women, a fact that can lead to rape and battery. Report these events when they happen.

2. Women's brains are equal in capacity to men's brains.

3. Know the record of women in action in government and society, in the past and today.

4. Know the issues that are important to women today.

5. For economic and mental-health reasons, support marriage and committed relationships.

6. Work to support the election of a woman president!

"Look for something positive within a situation that is disappointing and discouraging."

MARIETTA FORLAW, 96
Greensboro, North Carolina

- Born August 1920 in Greensboro, North Carolina
- Taught elementary school
- Member of the Religious Society of Friends (Quakers)
- Volunteered for YWCA, Guilford College, and American Friends Service Committee
- Has been a lifelong learner and budding artist

How the country recovered from challenging times

When the boys came back home from World War II, it was a very unsettling time. They had experienced a lot of new and different things while they were away, and it seemed that they were no longer given to the "old home ways." They stirred everything up.

At the same time, the returning soldiers brought fresh air and excitement with them. I remember that when the man I planned to marry came home from the War, I was teaching school in a small rural town where people were not well educated, and they were very set in their ways. I was getting discouraged in that environment. When Henry came home, he helped to lift me up with a broader perspective on things.

We got married in 1945. He didn't even have a suit of clothes to wear, and he had lost so much weight that his army uniform didn't fit. So he borrowed a uniform from a friend and wore it for our wedding.

After that, we lived in a boarding house with several other people. That was not ideal, but that was the only choice we had, and we were happy.

Marietta (left) in a photo she sent her future husband while he was overseas in World War II; with Henry Forlaw at their 1945 wedding

So, one bit of advice I would give to people today is to look for something positive within a situation that is disappointing and discouraging to you. There may be something you can hold onto that will help you move into a positive light. As in my experience with the boys coming home from the war, there are unsettling aspects, but there are also positive aspects. Seek the positive aspects and go forward with them.

When the country was at its best

When I was growing up in the 1920s and '30s, it was more common for many family members to live together in one household than it is today. In our home on Bragg Street in Greensboro, North Carolina, my aunt and two uncles lived with my father, mother, younger sister, and me. It seemed that all the adults had their own strong opinions about things, and many very lively conversations took place. My sister and I were not encouraged to join in, but we listened to everything. Sometimes we listened over the banister from the second floor of our big old house.

Everyone in our household was a Republican, except for Daddy, who was a Democrat. I remember when he was elected to the City Council. Later he became mayor pro tem of Greensboro. This was the time in my life when I felt the best about our country, because Daddy was part of the inner circle then, and I knew he was taking care of things.

I voted for the first time in 1944, and I voted for Franklin Roosevelt. I was 24 years old then, and I was teaching first grade in a small town in North Carolina. I was certainly old enough to form my own opinions about things. I did not vote Democratic because of my father, but of course, he had influenced my thinking about politics.

Advice for the country at this moment

Here is another perspective that I can share. One of the important things that Hillary Clinton said in her campaign is that we must come together and work together if we want to have a better world. I believe this is very true. I learned a lot about it when I was volunteering at the YWCA and the American Friends Service Committee in the 1960s and '70s. The key is to work together on positive projects. That's where you will get results. We cannot change the whole world at one time, even if that is the result we hope to see eventually. Do your best on projects and you can make good things happen.

"We have to stop thinking about hatred. We have to channel our anger to make things better."

BAILEY GORDON, 96
Riverdale, New York

- Born January 1920 in Chicago
- Voracious reader
- Successfully completes Sunday *New York Times* crossword weekly
- Mother, grandmother

How I have overcome personal setbacks

My husband's death was extremely difficult for me. It took me a while, but I finally started listening to music again. I thought of the good things I had in life because of him. Nobody gets over loss in a hurry; it takes time and effort. But you have to live again. You can't go on dwelling on your loss—it doesn't get you anywhere.

The best advice I ever got about recovering from difficult times

When I was 94, I was still living on my own in Florida. One day I fell, broke my hip, and had to have surgery. It was a very painful recovery, and I was quite depressed as I struggled through physical and occupational therapy. The best advice I received during this time was from my daughter and daughter-in-law: they encouraged me to take antidepressants.

How the country recovered from challenging times

Wars are horrible—horrible!—because you're

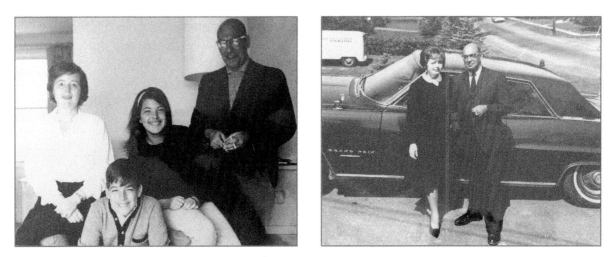

Bailey with husband, George, daughter, Shelley, and son, Alan, circa 1962 (top left); with husband, George, circa 1960 (top right); Bailey around age 22 (below)

never able to forget it. But I am a positive person. I always think things are going to get better.

My experiences with sexism and advice to young women

When I was working, people said some very hurtful remarks to me. I remember thinking, "You don't have to tolerate this. You have to speak up." I still feel that way.

Advice for the country at this moment

We have to stop thinking about hatred. We have to channel our anger to make things better. We cannot compromise on our values.

"The presence of God through the support I receive from friends helps even in the worst of times."

HELEN CANNAN GRAVES, 102
Buncombe County, North Carolina

- Born May 1914 in Eldorado, Illinois
- Went to the polls with her mother when women were first given the vote
- Mother told her: "Someday you will vote for a woman to be president."

How I have overcome personal setbacks

My early years were so secure and happy. Laughter, music, and good-natured teasing were in our home then. My little sister would play the clarinet and I would play the piano at church, school, or other community gatherings in our small Southern Illinois coal-mining town.

Our parents gave us a strong, positive attitude, and a good sense of humor, which helped when tragedies struck our family. The influenza epidemic of 1918 struck my mother especially hard. Shortly after a desperate move to El Paso, Texas, for clean air, my mother died when I was only twelve. My sister Mildred's appendix burst a few years later, and after a year of futile care in a hospital, she died, just a few years before penicillin could have cured her.

My mother appeared to me in a dream, holding two dresses—one blue and one white. When I reached out for the blue dress, my mother said that the blue dress was for Mildred; mine was the white dress. Mildred was buried in the blue dress.

Helen as a young woman and with Allen Graves, 1940

68

I have always thought of my wedding dress as the white dress Mother was speaking of in the dream.

Medical bills kept my father at work long hours, often accompanied by my little brother. The financial struggle of the Depression hit our family early, as my father's clients would pay with food they had grown, but little cash. The church and community provided support as they could.

After the tragic deaths, I cried until there were no more tears. I found that my Christian beliefs helped get me through the grief. I spent many hours alone at home, fantasizing about having a large family sitting around the table with a mother, father, and brothers and sisters laughing, talking, and sharing a meal together.

My dreams came true when I married my college sweetheart, and we eventually had six children sitting around our table. What a wonderful answer to my despair that was! Even at age 102, one of my favorite activities is sitting down at a table, surrounded by those I love, involved in a stimulating conversation filled with laughter.

The best advice I ever got about recovering from difficult times

The morning my husband died it was raining really hard. We had shared more than 50 years of marriage; the last ten he had suffered from Parkinson's. I heard a knock on the door. It was Henry Mugabe, a seminary student from Zimbabwe who is a dear friend of our family. No one had called Henry, but he just felt a special need that morning to come see us. We had taught in Nigeria after my husband had retired from his teaching duties at the seminary and felt especially close to students from Africa.

Helen with family, 1942

When Henry arrived, he told me that in his culture it is a very important sign if it is raining when a person dies. It means that the heavens themselves are weeping for the passing of a great man. Henry's words still give me such comfort. The special presence of God through the support I receive from friends like Henry helps so much even in the worst of times.

How the country recovered from challenging times

The 1960s were marked by social upheaval that challenged the heart of our nation. I tried to stay involved in what was going on in the world by living what I believed in. My husband was on a committee that invited Rev. Dr. Martin Luther King Jr. to speak at the seminary where he was the dean.

> *"I was out in my wheelchair at age 100 trying to give safe passage to women who needed an abortion."*

After Dr. King arrived he called our home, and we went to the airport to pick him up. That morning his sermon was a lot like the one he later gave that is known as his "I Have a Dream" speech. Dr. King was trying to inspire the white churches in the South to become more involved in the struggle for equal rights based on the biblical beliefs we shared as Christians.

I was shocked when so many people turned on us for inviting Dr. King. I was glad that our city brought churches together to support improved housing and schools.

The national outlook was bleak indeed after the assassination of President Kennedy and later of Dr. King and Bobby Kennedy. We continued the struggle by aligning ourselves with others in the community who supported the Civil Rights Act. I marched against the Vietnam War and wrote articles and church materials on improving race relations. I tried to give support to the neediest persons in our community.

Helen with Allen

My experiences with sexism and advice to young women

I felt discriminated against because of my gender many times, often in the church circles, where women were excluded from leadership of groups that included men. It wasn't until very late in my life that I was elected as the first woman to serve as a deacon in our church. Women just weren't allowed to do that back then.

I can remember in the 1930s going to a church meeting when the moderator called for my brother-in-law, a minister, to speak. His wife replied that he was outside in a committee meeting, but the moderator ruled her out of order since women were not allowed to speak. Now isn't that ridiculous?

Back when I had my first job after college, in the middle of the Great Depression, when I hardly had food to eat, I didn't receive the 50-dollar monthly stipend I was due. I think the man in charge thought he could keep it for himself since I was only a woman.

I also think that the horrible conditions that have developed around a woman's right to choose are a kind of sexism where others think they can

Helen marching in opposition to the Vietnam War

control a woman's own body. Again, I feel so strongly about this that I was out in my wheelchair from 7 to 9 a.m. at age 100 trying to give safe passage to the women who needed an abortion and had traveled many miles to one of the only two clinics in the state that would give them the medical care they needed. I was there with a dear family friend whose daughter had been desperate to have a child, but had to have a late-term abortion because of major life-threatening medical issues. Her daughter had to go through a gauntlet of hecklers to enter the clinic. Those hecklers were there the morning I sat in my wheelchair quietly guarding the entrance. I guess you would say my actions spoke loudly that morning.

I would rather not talk about the sexist remarks and actions of Trump. His campaign brought out what I think is the worst in America. I hated for my little great-granddaughters to hear some of the trash he was spouting off while they were trying to educate themselves by watching presidential debates and the evening news. I only hope America survives his presidency.

Advice for the country at this moment

Look to nature for inspiration. I always liked to have something growing in my yard: rose bushes at the corner window, a bank of irises along the driveway, peonies by the fountain. The stars at night are an amazing sight. Look to nature for rejuvenation of your spirit.

Take care of your personal responsibilities for things that have to be done. Don't expect others to do for you what you are able to do. Think of ways you can help others. If you can write, use your skill to challenge and inspire others. If you can speak, address your concerns to others. Read and pay attention to what is happening in your community. Help at the local schools, volunteer at the nursing homes, run for elective office, demonstrate for causes you believe in.

Remember what the country was founded on, and make sure you continue to exercise the constitutional rights and democratic principles that have held us together as a nation. Remember that we are here to safeguard nature for the next generation. Speak up, write, march for justice and peace and clean air and equality for women and people of all races and abilities.

The children are our future. Don't forget to care well for all our children.

"Run for elective office, demonstrate for causes you believe in."

GOLDIE GREENER, 98
Deerfield Beach, Florida

Goldie, Milton, and eldest son, Doug, 1945

- Born March 1918 in New York City
- In 1940 married Milton Greener, who served in the U.S. Army in Europe during World War II
- 2 sons, 3 grandsons, 2 great-grandsons

How the country recovered from challenging times

I was married in 1940. My husband Milton had a low number, so he was drafted very early, and he left for the army with me pregnant. I was living in the Bronx with my parents. The Army gave us 80 dollars a month, and sugar was rationed.

In February 1945 I got a telegram that Milton was missing in action. I lived for weeks not knowing if he was dead or alive, until I was informed that he had been taken captive in Germany. He lived in prison camps on potato-peel soup until he was liberated by the Army, sent to a hospital in France and then home to Fort Dix, New Jersey.

When Milton came home, you couldn't find any apartments for rent, and no new ones were being built. It was a terrible time, but we all believed the future would be better, that there would be no more wars. That's what got us through those difficult times.

When the country was at its best

They call us, the ones who lived through the war, the "Greatest Generation." I never used that term, but I think that that generation was the best. The war opened a lot of doors for women. They began working in factories and many other jobs that they never did before. We came through the Depression and the War, and we built a prosperous country.

"It was a terrible time, but we all believed the future would be better, that there would be no more wars."

KATHERINE BLOOD HOFFMAN, 102
Tallahassee, Florida

- Born August 1914 in Winter Haven, Florida
- Taught chemistry at Florida State College for Women and Florida State University for 44 years
- Dean of Women at FSU, where she constantly fought for women's rights

My experiences with sexism and advice to young women

I've always been conscious of the restrictions on women, but I didn't let it worry me too much. I've

Katherine receiving an honorary doctorate from Florida State University President T.K. Wetherell, 2007 (photo by Larry Halsey)

found if you do the job you're assigned, and do everything else you can, you'll make it all right.

When I graduated from Florida State College for Women, I applied and was accepted to the Duke University School of Medicine. Duke required that I sign a waiver promising not to marry while in their medical school. I wasn't even engaged, but I refused to sign because Duke didn't require the same promise from men. Instead, I chose to enter Columbia University, where I earned a Master of Arts degree in Chemistry.

In 1940, I moved back to Tallahassee and joined the faculty at Florida State College for Women, later coed Florida State University, where I taught chemistry until my retirement in 1984.

I advise young women to learn from the experiences of the people around them. The breadth of experience of others will benefit them when they apply it to their own situations, enabling them to take full advantage of the opportunities before them.

MARGARET HOLLISTER, 99
Washington, DC

- Born April 1917 in New York City
- Grew up in China, the eldest of 5 children of Presbyterian missionaries
- Worked as a teacher and social worker for many years, retiring in her mid-80s
- Wrote a memoir, *Inheriting China*, and her family's papers are in the Library of Congress
- Speaks Mandarin Chinese
- Still lives in her Capitol Hill home
- 2 sons, 3 grandchildren, 3 great-grandchildren

How I have overcome personal setbacks
Both of my sons protested against the Vietnam War. Those were awful years. My house was a safe house. People could store their cameras here, and they could store medicines. There were as many as 26 people—I think that was the most we had—who slept here, just head-to-toe on the living-room floor. The FBI was right across the street in a car.

One thing I learned growing up in China is there's just the next damn thing that comes along and you have to handle it.

The best advice I ever got about recovering from difficult times
I had a Scottish mother! My sisters and I were taught that our value was in being useful. We were supposed to work very hard; we were always supposed to have A's. She expected that.

I can't explain to you how sort of "just do it" my life was. I guess I must have been a stubborn young lady, because I don't remember much other advice that I took. There were rules, and you obeyed the rules. It wasn't a matter of specific advice.

How the country recovered from challenging times
I'm afraid that my wisdom as such is to just trust that you can handle the next thing when it comes. I think that's a pretty good philosophy, because then you don't waste any energy going back and saying, "Oh I wish I had done this, I wish I had done that." The only thing you have is the next thing. And I think that's a pretty solid place to be.

"I've never thought about gender in an election. All I've ever cared about was that somebody was competent and cared."

My experiences with sexism and advice to young women

In China when I was a child, everybody was always waiting for a boy. When a girl was born, it was universal sadness. They had a rhyme: "A dog is good around the house / A pig is useful too / A cat can always catch a mouse / But what's the use of a girl like you?"

I had three sisters and one brother. People would try to console my mother: "It's too bad, but maybe the next one will be a boy."

Mother had a very hard time at the birth of my brother. She was 40. I was called from boarding school, and I arrived at the mission hospital. My father was in the corridor, and a medical tech came up and congratulated him on his "firstborn." I'm 13 years old, and I'm standing there fresh from boarding school, and my father—who was raised in China—said thank you, accepted it, did not try to correct him, and didn't speak to me about it.

I can't express to you how much I think being raised in China left an imprint. But you just keep going. You just do the next thing, you take the next step, because that's the culture. That's really what you do.

Advice for the country at this moment

I think that at first you should accept the fact that you're in shock. I did. I said, "I'm giving myself a week to not try to make sense of anything." And then slowly I felt the need to belong to something, so I signed up with Bernie Sanders' group, Our Revolution.

I choose the thing that is closest to my ideals. For example, I do believe in honesty. I would recommend to people that they do the honest thing,

Margaret as a student at Yenching University, China, age 17, 1934

whatever the honest thing is for them.

First of all, you listen to what's going on—what can you support and what can you not? And then if there's something you can't support, you try to find some people who also don't support it, and join up in some way. You have to listen. You have to evaluate. And I think we need other people. To think of yourself as being alone is a hard thing.

I've never thought about gender in an election. All I've ever cared about was that somebody was competent and cared. I haven't given a hoot about whether they were men or women. When I became politically aware, there had been Queen Victoria for 50 years and also the Empress dowager, who was very powerful in China, for about 50 years. So I was quite accustomed to women being in charge of things. I voted for Hillary Clinton because I couldn't possibly vote for the other one. No, I did not vote for her because she was a woman. I wouldn't. I would never.

"I learned that I could take care of myself, that I didn't need a man to take care of me."

HELEN ROBERSON HUNTER, 97
Oro Valley, Arizona

- Born July 1919 in Atchison County, Missouri
- Farmed with husband in rural northwest Missouri, conserving the land and producing food
- Has always advocated for an inclusive and generous society
- Role model in exemplifying kindness and understanding
- 2 daughters, 6 grandchildren, 11 great-grandchildren

The best advice I ever got about recovering from difficult times

My most helpful advice came from my dad. He always said, "This too shall pass." I have found this to be a good way to approach problems. Keep trying, don't give up, and things will work out eventually.

Helen at age two

Helen as a college student (top) and with her husband, Marion Hunter, around the time of their marriage

When the country was at its best

The country was at its best for me when my life was happy and peaceful. That was when my kids were little, and I was a homemaker and mother. We were living on the farm in Missouri, and I was mowing the lawn, working in 4-H, and tending the garden. I was busy with meaningful and satisfying work. It seemed that people were generally kinder to each other, and emphasized similarities and the common good over personal differences.

Advice for the country at this moment

I was lucky to be able to graduate college because my dad could afford it, and my family, especially my older brother, thought it was very important. He also wanted me to go away to school—far enough away to be on my own and experience new things.

By having an education and a job (beginning with a one-room schoolhouse), I learned that I could take care of myself, that I didn't need a man to take care of me. Knowledge like that brings great freedom and security—especially to women. Of course, I did marry and have twin daughters, but I never lost my feeling of self-confidence.

So, advice to young people: learn as much as you can, and experience the world as much as you can. Your knowledge will enrich your family and your community. You will make wise choices. You will help others. You can live a life you will be proud of.

ROSE KAUFMAN, 102
Santa Monica, California

- Born January 1914 in Philadelphia, Pennsylvania
- Moved with her husband, an engineer, to Toledo, Ohio, in 1950 and to Santa Monica, California, in 1960
- Active in League of Women Voters since 1951, serving two terms as chapter president
- Served on city's commission on older adults, a hospital's ethics committee, and a group overseeing a community college's program for older adults

How I have overcome personal setbacks

I was the fifth child. The first was a boy, then my three sisters, and me. In 1924, my beloved brother passed away after a four-day battle with spinal meningitis. Sulfa and penicillin weren't available then. My older sisters comforted me, and we strengthened each other. My mother fell into a deep depression. My father was devastated but still tried to help us cope. It was a traumatic experience for a ten-year-old. I think that marked all of us seriously in different ways.

The best advice I ever got about recovering from difficult times

Keeping busy, doing volunteer work, and speaking up where you see bigotry or unwelcome behavior should be part of everyday living. To live a long life, keep breathing. To live a meaningful life, keep doing.

How the country recovered from challenging times

The Great Depression of the '30s was probably the deepest mark of all. My father's thriving clothing manufacturing business collapsed. My mother did not comprehend a changed economy. We were never hungry, but I knew families who were. My sister gave her coat to a girl who had none.

Everyone made a supreme effort. After the '30s, laws were passed. There were many lessons to be learned about loans, credit, and inflation. The Great Depression was much more severe than the recent crisis.

"To live a long life, keep breathing. To live a meaningful life, keep doing."

My experiences with sexism and advice to young women

I have long felt that men were more valued than women, boy babies more welcome than girl babies. Part of that was because the boys were wage earners, and the women were never prepared for a job and weren't able to work. Parents thought it was more important to see that boys had a college education than girls. Many mothers indoctrinated their children with the goal to marry a rich man, or one who was a good wage earner. There were women who wanted to go to college. A few did, and a few got degrees. But even then, schools never wanted girl students. The deans said that women would get the degree and then get married, so they wanted nothing to do with that.

It all made me feel that there were some things I simply couldn't do. I was just told, "Don't worry about it." I graduated high school in 1930 at age 16. I had witnessed my sister Etta's heartbreak two years earlier because college was not her next step. After the Depression some girls went to college and worked at the same time, working as a waitress and paying their own way. I felt I couldn't do that.

I didn't go to college, but eventually found a job and I was quite proud. I made 12 dollars a week and gave my mother 5 dollars a week. It was a very common practice. In the '30s, women who got married often still did work to give money to their parents.

Things are different now, although change has been slow. I remember an undercurrent of

Rose with two of her three children

an effort to establish women's rights. World War II changed things, because women went to work in men's jobs. Rosie the Riveter was praised. The social scene has changed because of the efforts of Betty Friedan and others. Things are different because of Carrie Chapman Catt and the League of Women Voters. People started to believe that women could participate as well as men.

My advice to women is that they should believe they are equal to men. They should try to establish something that would give them a way to earn a living and be independent: live alone, manage her own money, and be equal to the men. And feel independent.

Personally, I think that self-esteem is what we need. And I mean self-esteem on an equal basis to the male competition.

Advice for the country at this moment

The only advice I can suggest is to have a goal and keep working at it, and take the disappointments as they come along and keep working at it. We do have social changes, but it takes a long time. Ultimately, we shall overcome.

"I don't remember feeling I was ever at a disadvantage for being a woman."

ALICE "LAL" COXE KEITH, 97
Clarkdale, Arizona

- Born April 1919 in Buffalo, New York
- Twin of Cornelia "Neal" Coxe Brewster
- Worked as church secretary for 16 years
- Lifelong Democrat
- 6 children, 6 grandchildren,
  1 great-grandchild

How I have overcome personal setbacks
When my husband died at age 53, that was the hardest time for me. I got a lot of help from the people at the church where I was working. And then those of my kids who were in and out during the time after his death helped me get through it.

How the country recovered from challenging times
Growing up, the most difficult time was during the Depression. We had no money but had to buy clothes to go to our jobs. I had two outfits

Coxe girls: Cornelia, Alice, Adelaide, and their mother, Alice, late 1920's

to go to work and one for church. Some of my parents' friends who were better off helped us as they could, and my mother figured out various ways to make a little money and stretch the little that we did have.

It was also hard during the war, but it wasn't just us—it affected everyone, and we were all part of a big effort. When we were stationed in Oregon with no family around, that was hard. Going to church helped me during that time also, as well as other couples, most of whom did not yet have children. Some of them would babysit occasionally, particularly when my second child was born.

When the country was at its best
After the war was over, people cheered up and figured they had been through the worst—the Depression and World War II—and there was just a better outlook.

My experiences with sexism and advice to young women
I just don't remember feeling I was ever at a disadvantage for being a woman. Between my jobs and the equality I felt with my husband, I didn't ever feel like a victim of sexism.

Advice for the country at this moment
There will be another election in four years. Young people should stay involved and be sure to vote.

Alice in 1940 (top) (photo by her twin sister, Cornelia [Neal] Coxe Brewster); with Neal around 1970

"Knowing that my children will continue my passion for politics gives me comfort."

ROSELYN KRAUS, 99
Skokie, Illinois

Roselyn at 18 months

- Born June 1917 in Chicago
- Walked precinct with twins in baby buggy more than 6 decades ago
- Passed along passion for politics to children
- Still lives independently

How I have overcome personal setbacks

I recall the two most painful periods of trauma in my life, one as a child growing up during the Depression. We always had food to eat, and my mother was a creative cook and baker. But clothes were another matter. Fortunately, I had older cousins who passed along their outgrown clothes to me. I remember we were given white fabric and patterns in elementary-school sewing class with which to make our graduation dresses. Because I had uncles who were tailors, they helped me at home, and my dress turned out better than anything I could have made alone.

We suffered much more excruciating pain when, as parents, we lost a child through illness. It is more in the natural order of life for adults to lose a parent than to lose their own child. My husband and I survived by leaning on each other emotionally while we also tried to help our daughters cope as well. My husband of 63 years was always my rock and the love of my life. Family, friends, and our faith in God were always there as well to help.

Advice for the country at this moment

Now we try to comfort our daughters over the loss of Hillary Clinton in our recent election. They are still crying, and we tell them that this too shall pass. When Adlai Stevenson lost the election for president in 1956, we took them to meet him at his farm in Libertyville, Illinois. We took comfort in his gracious welcome. I remember his quote in defeat: "It hurts too much to laugh, but I'm too old to cry." Knowing that my children will continue my passion for politics gives me comfort. I only wish they didn't have to deal with futures framed by Trump.

I saw Barack Obama speaking at the Democratic convention in 2004, and I immediately said to my family that he will one day be our president. I hoped I would still be alive to see it. Now I have seen it. I hoped that I would get to see Hillary Clinton as our first woman president. Nonetheless, I've had a wonderful life filled with much joy, precious family and friends. Truly, no one ever promised me a rose garden, but I consider myself a very lucky lady. God has been so good to me.

Roselyn in a coat made by her uncles during the Depression (top) and at 23 with her future husband

PEARL KREPCHIN, 97
Rockville, Maryland

- Born October 1919 in New York City
- Worked for the Office of Price Administration and War Department during World War II
- Taught kindergarten
- 2 children, 3 grandchildren, 1 great-grandchild

How the country recovered from challenging times

One of the most hopeful periods I remember was when FDR was president and he started the WPA. All kinds of projects were going on: new roads and bridges. And I remember a real spirit of cooperation in the country, even though there were some who ridiculed the efforts. There was a song describing the successes of the program, and the chorus was "… and we did it all while leaning on a shovel."

And the good works and example set by Eleanor Roosevelt also helped the recovery from the Depression. I tend to be an optimist and see the brighter side of things, which can help in times of trouble, both personal and national.

During World War II, I worked in the Office of Price Administration and felt like I was doing useful work.

"When FDR was president, I remember a real spirit of cooperation in the country."

Pearl in 1943

"Sometimes the most dislikable creatures will turn out to surprise you."

PATRICIA LIGHTBODY, 97
Chagrin Falls, Ohio

♦ Born March 1919 in Newton, Massachusetts

How I have overcome personal setbacks
Get out of bed, and put one foot in front of the other.

The best advice I ever got about recovering from difficult times
This too shall pass. (Repeated frequently at the dinner table.)

How the country recovered from challenging times
Up and at 'em.

When the country was at its best
Our country has never been at its best. There are better times ahead in the future.

My experiences with sexism and advice to young women
Education is most important. It frees women to accomplish great things.

Advice for the country at this moment
Sometimes the most dislikable creatures will turn out to surprise you.

Patricia in 1938

EMILY LUKASIK, 98
Ferndale, Michigan

- Born September 1918 in Pittsburgh, Pennsylvania
- Helped World War II effort as a "Rosie," sewing seat cushions for General Motors
- Was married for over 50 years
- 3 children, 10 grandchildren, 24 great-grandchildren, 2 great-great-grandchildren

How I have overcome personal setbacks
I lost my husband, brothers and sister, my mother and father, a daughter, and a granddaughter. I cried and kept busy. I tried not think about losses. I kept moving.

How the country recovered from challenging times
People pulled up their bootstraps and did what they had to. They managed. The government helped people through the hard times. We lived with family when we had to, and we worked together.

Emily at age 6 with brothers, Eddie, a few months old, and Al, age 8

When the country was at its best
When World War II ended and the soldiers were coming home, people were laughing and crying.

Advice for the country at this moment
Work with the new president, and do what you have to to keep the country strong. If something is wrong, speak up. The Electoral College? They can shove it. It has to change!

"Do what you have to to keep the country strong. If something is wrong, speak up."

"I was raised to believe that everyone should have equal rights. But many doors were closed to women and people of color."

BEATRICE LUMPKIN, 98
Chicago, Illinois

- Born August 1918 in New York City
- Labor activist for 83 years
- Officer of Chicago Metro Retirees, part of the Illinois Alliance for Retired Americans
- Founding member of Coalition of Labor Union Women
- 4 children, 3 grandchildren, 1 great-grandchild, 3 honorary great-great-grandchildren

How the country recovered from challenging times

The national outlook seemed very bleak in 1930, when I was 12 years old. The unemployment figure was around 25 percent, but in my neighborhood it was higher. And there was no government welfare, so people were dying from

Beatrice, age 5, 1923

"We older people will help you turn our country around. Let's form a grand new intergenerational alliance for progress."

Beatrice and Frank Lumpkin, 1950
(photo by Joe Banks)

the effects of hunger.

But the unemployed organized to demand jobs. The communists and the socialists deserve a lot of credit for that. They won public welfare after one million unemployed marched to their state capitols on March 6, 1930.

Some of my neighbors were in that Hunger March. What I learned from that experience was, "It pays to organize."

In high school, I joined the fight for unemployment insurance and social security. In college, I took a year off as an organizer for the new CIO (Committee for Industrial Organization). They were organizing factory workers—black, brown, white, men, women—breaking down divisions by race, gender, or language.

And we had a president, FDR, who responded to the people. His huge public works jobs projects brought hope to millions. The WPA alone, in just a few months, put 4 million to work on useful projects and lifted the whole economy. That was the New Deal. It eased the suffering, expanded our rights, improved the nation's infrastructure, and gave us hope.

The key to our recovery had two parts. First, millions of people organized and united, overcoming racism, sexism, anti-immigrant bias, and red-baiting. The other part was the election of President Franklin D. Roosevelt and a Congress that adopted the New Deal, providing a safety net.

My experiences with sexism and advice to young women

I first became aware of sexism as a little girl. Handball was a big sport in the Bronx, where I grew up. But it was considered a male sport. Fortunately for me, my parents never told me that I could not do something because I was a girl. So I did not give up. I waited until the boys were one player short and no boy was available. Then they let me play. Sometimes I even got reluctant praise.

I was raised to believe that everyone should have equal rights. But many doors were closed to women and people of color. I was not allowed to major in physics in college. That's because the free city colleges in Manhattan had separate schools for men and women, and only the men's college offered a physics major.

In 1949, I was fired from two jobs for being pregnant. As late as 1964 my boss told me, "For what I'm paying you, I could get a man." Then he fired me and gave my job to a man I had trained! Happily, in 1965 the Civil Rights Act was passed and outlawed that type of open sexism. Based on my experience, I think that it pays to fight for your rights. That's the way we can win equality.

Advice for the country at this moment

I believe that young people will lead our country toward a better, more humane society. My message to them is: don't waste time grieving the 2016 Electoral College defeat of the first female major party candidate to run for president. Instead, organize and continue to fight for the rights of the 99 percent. We older people will help you turn our country around. Let's form a grand new intergenerational alliance for progress.

That's what I witnessed during the Great Depression. For 99 percent of young people, the

Beatrice and her friend Katie Jordan protesting with Coalition of Labor Union Women outside Democratic Party Convention, Chicago, 1996

future looked dismal in 1936. But young people built movements to win jobs or compensation for the unemployed. They were the leaders in bringing together the unemployed councils, the civil rights and women's movements, and the new industrial unions.

For example, in 1936, the national president of UE (United Electrical, Radio and Machine Workers of America), then a large CIO union, was only 25 years old. Not too long ago we saw the Occupy movement speak up for the 99 percent and change the national conversation. And I predict that young people will continue the Bernie Sanders revolution and prevent fascist-minded right-wing Republicans from plunging our country into hell.

"My mother told me, 'Find someone worse off than you, and go help them and cheer them up.'"

ELIBET KÜNZLER MARSHALL, 99
La Jolla, California

- Born June 1917 in Urfa, Turkey
- Grew up in Beirut, where her parents worked with Armenian refugee children
- Came to U.S. as a Goucher College exchange student
- Married an American medical student in Beirut, returning to U.S. at start of World War II
- Artist, teacher, prize-winning succulent grower
- 4 daughters, 5 grandchildren, 2 great-grandchildren

How I have overcome personal setbacks

When I was a young child, my parents were medical missionaries, working for Near East Relief in the last days of the Ottoman Empire. During the Armenian genocide, they rescued eight thousand Armenian orphan children by walking with them from present-day Turkey, through Syria, to Lebanon, where they settled them in orphanages.

Elibet (third from right), age 2, with family in 1919

90

During this time, there was no word from my parents, so they were presumed dead. My sisters and I lived in an orphanage in Switzerland. I was very young and sad and missed my parents so much. My oldest sister became my "mother," and I would not have survived without her. From this, I learned the importance of family taking care of each other.

And then my parents came back, and we heard about the hardships of the children they saved, who had no parents to care for them. So, I learned one of the most important things to help you through life is a caring family and a stable home. My parents spent the rest of their lives making homes and schools for the orphans they rescued, some of whom became my brothers and sisters, too.

The best advice I ever got about recovering from difficult times

When I was a foreign-exchange student from Beirut at Goucher College, in Maryland, I was very homesick. My mother told me that feeling sorry for yourself is selfish. "Look around," she'd say. "Find someone worse off and more homesick than you, and go help them and cheer them up."

My experiences with sexism and advice to young women

I always wanted to be an architect or artist or journalist. Papa insisted that men, not women, became architects or journalists, and to become

Elibet, age 17, 1934

an artist you had to bed down with a lot of men to make it to the top.

I saw what I must do: I must become a teacher and spearhead the movement to relax outdated rules, which constrained and restricted young women. And I raised my four daughters to know they could do anything they wanted to do. You are responsible for your own life and happiness. No one can do it for you— no single religion or living space. I tell young women now to work hard and be honest and true to yourself.

LILLIAN HELEN DOUGLASS SCHOENSTEIN COLLINS MCCOSKEY, 97
Madison, Indiana

- Born November 1919 in Madison, Indiana

Lillian with first husband John Schoenstein around 1947

How I have overcome personal setbacks

The worst thing that happened to me is when I lost my daughter when I was 95. Or when I lost my first husband from cancer. He was the love of my life. In my life, I've had many setbacks, but I realized that there is nothing I can do but keep going.

When the country was at its best

The best time was under Reagan. He always seemed to be in good humor when he addressed the nation.

My experiences with sexism and advice to young women

I never had any problems with sexism. I agreed with everyone, then did what I pleased. My advice is to be true to yourself, and if you don't like it, don't do it.

Advice for the country at this moment

I've lived many years, and you don't know what's going to happen tomorrow. Tomorrow may be better, or it may be worse. If you don't like it, don't worry. It will change eventually.

"Tomorrow may be better, or it may be worse. If you don't like it, don't worry. It will change eventually."

"The more educated you are, the more you learn to understand and respect other people."

MAY MIREL, 97
Thousand Oaks, California

- Born November 1919 in Czernowitz, Austria-Hungary
- Naturalized in the U.S. as infant
- Bachelor's degree in accounting from City College of New York; master's degrees in urban education and early childhood education from Brooklyn College
- Accountant; medical assistant to first husband; New York City elementary school teacher; legal assistant to second husband
- Married and widowed from two terrific husbands; also lost a close companion
- 3 children, many grandchildren and great-grandchildren

How I have overcome personal setbacks

The first time I experienced tragedy was when my first husband, Julian, died from Hodgkin's disease after ten years of illness. I was left a widow with three children. I wished to die, but I knew I had children to take care of. I had been working with my husband's medical practice, so now I needed to get a different job. I went back to Brooklyn College for a master's degree in urban education. I was hired as an early child-hood teacher at PS 202, where I worked for 16 years. I will forever remember and admire my principal, Mr. Taffler, because he let me take my lunch during my students' lunchtime so I

May at college graduation and in the 1960s

could leave work at 2:30 p.m. and be home in time for my daughter to get home from school.

The best advice I ever got about recovering from difficult times

You have to be strong. You have to realize that life is not easy, that you will have many disappointments, and you have to try to overcome them. I gave myself this advice, and I told it to myself every time I got scared.

How the country recovered from challenging times

I remember when Senator Joseph McCarthy was trying to silence dissent. He was so terrible. And I remember Edward R. Murrow and Attorney Joseph Welch having the courage to speak up. When Attorney Welch challenged McCarthy's decency, I admired him tremendously, and I felt that was a turning point, and our country would recover.

When the country was at its best

The country was at its best during Obama's presidency because he inspired us, treating everyone as being equal. He is a great man, a great speaker, and I have tremendous respect for him and his wife. He inspires hope and love for all people, and he values education. To me, education is the secret to all things good, because the more educated you are, the more you learn to understand and respect other people, and the more you are able to reason with them, even when you may not agree with their opinion.

Advice for the country at this moment

Have hope. Vote. Express your opinion. March. Keep challenging the new administration, as The *New York Times* is doing.

"You don't get everything you want when you want it, but eventually it will come."

LAURA NEELMAN, 104
Patchogue, New York

- Born January 1912 in New York City
- Loves her family, reading, and chocolate
- 2 children, 5 grandchildren, 7 great-grandchildren

Advice for the country at this moment
I remember when I was about seven I got an umbrella for my birthday. I couldn't wait for the rain to come along so I could use that umbrella. And it didn't rain, and it didn't rain!

Of course, it did eventually. You don't get everything you want when you want it, but eventually it will come.

Laura and her parents (left); Laura (top row right) and her sisters, Lillian, Ruthie, and Helen, surrounding her mother, Fannie; Laura in the 1940s (right)

Photo of Miriam by Eduard Pastor

"I was up for a job as a choreographer for Elvis Presley, but he said he didn't want to work with a girl."

MIRIAM NELSON, 97
Beverly Hills, California

- Born September 1919 in Chicago
- Danced in six Broadway shows, starting in 1939
- Choreographed for Judy Garland, Carol Channing, and Anne Miller, among others
- Choreographed for movies including *Breakfast at Tiffany's, The Jolson Story, Picnic,* and *The Apartment*
- Conceived and staged shows for Radio City Music Hall, the Hollywood Bowl, the opening of Madison Square Garden, and Super Bowl Halftime Show
- Was a founder of SHARE (Share Happily and Reap Endlessly), a women's group that raised funds for developmentally disabled and abused children

How I have overcome personal setbacks

When I was very young, I auditioned to be a Rockette at Radio City Music Hall. The chore- ographer said to me, "You're capable of doing it all, but come back when you grow up." I used to get that all the time: "Come back when you grow up."

Years later, I choreographed a big number for the Academy Awards show. The people at Radio City saw it and called me. They asked if I would stage that number with their company of dancers for the Easter show. I said I would, and I did. After we finished rehearsing, I let everybody go, and I was the only one left. As I was picking up my purse and a few things, I remember looking out at that humongous, empty hall, all those empty seats. I thought, I guess I've grown up.

The best advice I ever got about recovering from difficult times

My hairdresser once told me she had gone to

Miriam, dancer and choreographer (Rusty Frank Archive)

a wonderful meeting and recommended it: Science of Mind. So I went to hear Dr. Robert Bitzer. I thought he was speaking just to me. It was *that* personal and made such an impression. I've been part of Science of Mind ever since.

It's all about positive thinking. I think that's important. I've been so aware, more aware lately, of negative people who seem to thrive on negative things. I think you attract what you put out. If you put out negative, you're going to get it back. That's my theory. No matter what goes on, I try to make it positive.

How the country recovered from challenging times

I remember hearing about the Depression, but I never felt it. I was busy. I was working. My mother had a little job, and we were never hungry. I heard about people being hungry. I never was.

When the country was at its best

I relate to the '40s and '50s because it was good for me. I was working, I was happy, I was going to tap school, and I was busy.

My experiences with sexism and advice to young women

I was up for a job as a choreographer for Elvis Presley, but he said he didn't want to work with a girl. He would be embarrassed not to pick up the steps, or whatever was required of him. He said he would rather have a fellow. He'd just feel more comfortable.

There weren't many other female choreographers back then. I always tried to be easy

Publicity photos of Miriam (Rusty Frank Archive)

to work with. I never tried to make somebody dance like I dance. I would watch them, and then I would try to teach them something that I could see would work on their body. I never tried to force anything on them. I tried to make them look good at what they could do.

My advice to young women: Keep doing what you're doing. Don't ever get discouraged. Don't give up. Persevere. Just keep going, and it'll happen for you. If you have the talent, it'll come out.

Advice for the country at this moment
I think we have to wait it out, and then Trump's going to show his hand one day. I mean, he's made so many mistakes, I don't know why people can't see that. I really don't.

As for advice, don't ever give up. Don't sit down. You have to stand up! Keep going every day. You just have to hang in there.

"Male faculty members and students did not take women as seriously as they did males. I persevered by trying to be the best—at everything."

MARY ELIZABETH NORTON, 103
Ithaca, New York

- Born September 1913 in Ann Arbor, Michigan
- Daughter of Irish immigrants
- Earned bachelor's and master's degrees from the University of Michigan
- Taught Classics at George Washington University for 20 years
- 2 children

How the country recovered from challenging times

During the Depression, times were very bleak. We lived in Ann Arbor, and my mother took in college-student roomers, whom I recruited on campus. We grew vegetables in our large back yard. I sold them door to door to make money and bought candy bars for three cents at the grocery store and sold them for five cents each at fraternity houses. I also sold other things door to door. I never knew I was deprived because everyone else was experiencing the same problems. Working hard together helped everyone get through it; and we enjoyed small pleasures, for example, five-cent hamburgers or ten-cent ice cream cones. The key to our recovery was never abandoning the ideal of democracy in the toughest times.

When the country was at its best

The U.S. was at its best in the Kennedy and Johnson years, before the assassinations of Robert Kennedy and Martin Luther King in 1968 and the expansion of the Vietnam War.

My experiences with sexism and advice to young women

I was a straight-A student and Phi Beta Kappa in Classics and History at the University of Michigan (class of 1935). No professor (all of them male) ever said to me that I should think about furthering my education and earning a PhD to teach in college. Therefore, although I later taught in college, I only had an MA, which I earned in three summers while teaching high school before my marriage. During the Depression, married women could not be employed as teachers in most states, so that the jobs could be reserved for men, who were viewed as appropriate family breadwinners. When I started teaching in college, I could tell that male faculty members and students did not take women as seriously as they did male colleagues or instructors. I persevered by trying to be the best—at everything!

Mary at University of Michigan graduation, 1935

"In the Civil Rights movement, black people were absolutely right in their protests for equality." —Mae Belle

"You need to find something to do that can please you and can help other people." —Mary

MAE BELLE POWELL AND MARY BELLE ROACH, 100
Symsonia, Kentucky

- Born March 1916 in Symsonia, Kentucky, in the same house they now share
- First women in their family to attend college, graduating from Murray State University in 1937
- Married best friends and moved to Detroit during World War II
- During World War II, Mae Belle worked on B-57 airplanes, and Mary built Jeep carburetors
- Both taught fifth and sixth grade for 42 years (Mae Bell, history; Mary, social studies)
- Mary has 1 daughter and 1 granddaughter, Mae Belle had 2 sons

Mae Belle Powell and Mary Roach

MAE BELLE POWELL

How I have overcome personal setbacks

I would overcome it by asking the Lord to help me, and He did. By going to the Lord and telling Him my troubles, and He took care of me. I pray for Donald Trump every night that he will be able to be the president of the United States.

The best advice I ever got about recovering from difficult times

Try to go on with your life. Set your troubles aside and go on. If I thought the advice would help me, I would try it. If not, I would ignore it.

How the country recovered from challenging times

With the WPA President Roosevelt would give poor people a job, such as building roads and bridges and things of that sort. And some of the farmers in our community— if you had a wagon and a horse, they would pay you a

The Wallace Family: Ernest, Virginia, Grace, Mary, and Mae Belle

dollar a day to haul gravel. This was at the beginning of the Depression in 1930.

In terms of the war, I very much value my experience of being in a factory. I had never been in a factory before; I had always been in school. I got to see how the rest of the world lived.

There was a story I heard of an incident on a streetcar. A black man jumped on the streetcar during the riots; he was being chased by a crowd of white men. And when he got on the streetcar, a white woman called him over and had him kneel down behind her and she had on a really big skirt. She wrapped her skirt around him, and when the men got on to attack him, everyone on the car said that they hadn't seen him. She saved his life. I think that's a great story of people protecting each other, strangers.

And in terms of the civil rights movement, black people were absolutely right in their protests for equality. I believe that Martin Luther King Jr. helped his people and he loved them. These people had the right idea and they changed the world. Don't forget that.

When the country was at its best

I liked the 1980s because I traveled all over the world. And things were in really good shape then.

My experiences with sexism and advice to young women

Get an education!

Mae Belle and Mary in their college yearbook

MARY BELLE ROACH

How I have overcome personal setbacks

The death of our families. I turn to my church family. I wouldn't know what to do without my church family. Everyone needs a "family," a group of people who think like you and can support you in difficult times. My advice would be to create a family of people who you can share with and who support you.

I would say I was disappointed with the election, and four years from now I would try again to get the Democratic Party back in focus. This will pass.

The best advice I ever got about recovering from difficult times

For me it was a tragedy when my husband, Wallace, died. One day I went to visit my neighbor Josephine Draffen, and she was quilting a beautiful orange quilt. Wallace had died, and my daughter was grown, and Mae Belle still had her husband, Loman, to take care of, and I was all by myself. Josephine told me, "You need to find something to do that can please you and can help other people." I said, "I wish that I could do that." And she said, "I will show you how."

And she did. We call them love quilts, and we made over one hundred of them and gave them away to all of our friends. We gave them to church charities, and if the fire department had a fundraiser, we gave them a quilt. Our church had a fundraiser, The Methodist Women, and we gave them a quilt. So I spent hours and hours quilting. I enjoyed it, and other people enjoyed it.

Oh, and from my daddy: "Always tell the truth."

How the country recovered from challenging times

I would say, the Depression. And the president was the most wonderful person in the whole world that came through with jobs for everyone. We were in college during the Depression, and my daddy borrowed money from the bank, and my grandfather owned a grocery store that fed us and helped us with our college money.

During World War II, we worked. And for me, World War II was fun; we had lots of fun! My Lord, we went to Detroit, and we had never seen an opera. We had never seen good music. We ate out, we traveled around; we had lots of fun. We also lived in Detroit during the race riots. On Belle Isle, there were fires, there were shotguns, there was burning of cars, and people turning over cars.

The worst day of my life, in terms of politics, was the day John Kennedy was assassinated. He really represented all the best of America to me, things we worked for. I knew the whole country was in for a setback because he was the one politician who could do the job we needed. I think now people feel the same way because Hillary was not elected. But Hillary hasn't died; there is still much she will do!

When the country was at its best

Bill Clinton! He did for everybody. Especially for my granddaughter! He helped her to get her citizenship papers (she is internationally adopted). I liked him. There wasn't anything I disliked about him. I liked the way he knew exactly what to do and when to do it. He treated everybody fairly. And he had the smartest wife that was ever qualified for anything!

My experiences with sexism and advice to young women

When I was a schoolteacher, our principal bossed us around all the time. I usually just ignored him. But one time, I confronted him. And that was when he was whipping those boys in the gym. Well, he had them whip each other. He made them cut their own switches, and he made all the students go to the gym to watch them whip each other like a prizefight.

I went down to his office, and I said, "That's enough of that." And he said, "Shut up and get out of here or I'll give you some of what they're getting." And I said, "Go ahead." And then I got up and walked out.

Then, in World War II, we were making carburetors for Ford Jeeps. It was all women on the second shift. And on the first shift, it was all men. The men made one thousand carburetors a day, and the women made three thousand. And the steward came around and said, "You're killing this job. You're making the men look bad."

This one woman I worked with, this Jewish woman, had eight boys in the war. She said, "I'm not doing this for me and you, or anyone else. I'm doing it for my boys." And we kept making three thousand carburetors a day.

My advice to girls is: get yourself the best education in the whole world, and never let any man ever boss you around or control you.

Advice for the country at this moment

Next time vote for a Democrat! And walk by faith, not by sight, and God will take care of it.

"During the Depression, my grandmother would often make us potato soup, nothing but potatoes and water."

ELIZABETH PULA, 97
New York City

- Born February 1919 in New York City
- Raised by relatives during the Depression
- Spent 7 years in tuberculosis hospitals
- Wasn't able to attend college, but has grandsons at Stanford and Yale Universities and granddaughters who attended Vassar and Bryn Mawr
- Educated herself through her curiosity and doing crossword puzzles
- Uses a computer and Skypes
- 3 children, 7 grandchildren, 5 great-grandchildren

How I have overcome personal setbacks
When I learned I had tuberculosis at 22, I cried and cried. They said I had to rest for six months, and I was so upset. Then that turned into almost seven years. That was the big turning point in

my life. I learned to be patient. I took nothing for granted after that. I don't consider it a bad experience, because I lived.

I was safely in a sanitarium during World War II, and my husband came to visit—he brought a Christmas tree one year, carried on the train! I saw so many beautiful young people die, the most beautiful girl I ever saw, and there was nothing that could be done to save them. I never envied anyone after that. I thought, *Here I am!*

When I left Lenox Hill Hospital to go to the san, the head nurse told me she never thought she would see me walk out alive. That's a heck of a thing to hear when you are 23. When I finally got out (at age 29), I couldn't return home because I couldn't walk up to our fourth-floor apartment, so we had to get another apartment that was more accessible. Before I got sick, I used to roller skate around Manhattan, and, instead of smoking cigarettes on my lunch break when I started working, I would go ice skating in Central Park. Maybe that helped me stay alive.

The best advice I ever got about recovering from difficult times

I didn't have any sages in my family to advise me, so I learned mostly by example. I tried to find people who seemed to do the right thing. My grandmother Johanna Hodum Schluter always saved for a rainy day, so I got that from her.

Even though I was not Jewish, I had heard that the Jews would take good care of their sick. So when I had TB, I chose a Jewish sanitarium over a state-run one, and that is probably why I am alive today.

After I recovered, I was happy to be alive and never was materialistic after that. I realized God made us all, and when you are sick, it doesn't matter who you are; rich or poor, no favors are paid.

How the country recovered from challenging times

For me, the bleakest time was growing up during the Depression. We would wonder what we were going to eat. My grandmother would often make us potato soup, nothing but potatoes and water. My aunt was a factory worker when they were trying to improve conditions and went on strike. We had no food at home and went to a Catholic church to ask if they would give us any food. The priest told my aunt to go back to work and wouldn't give us anything!

We didn't know when it was going to end. But we managed. We got by with what we had. But we had hope that things were going to change. We all felt like we were in it together. That's important.

Elizabeth as a young woman

"I loved my job, but my husband said it was the worst thing that ever happened, because after that I had too many opinions."

When the country was at its best

I hate to say it, but when Eisenhower was president, the war was over, times were good, the Marshall Plan was in Europe, everyone was happy and that is when my children were born. They were quiet years. People seemed to feel they had a future, and they were optimistic.

That was all true under JFK also, but that ended when he was killed.

My experiences with sexism and advice to young women

I went back to work at 47, in 1967, to earn money for my daughter's college education, which my husband didn't think was necessary; he just saved for my son's college. I had no experience except five years as a Girl Scout leader and helping my kids with their homework. But that helped me pass the aptitude tests! I worked at trucking companies in credit and collections. I had to ask one of my employers to take down the topless girlie pictures in the drivers' break room. They did! One of the drivers made a union grievance because he didn't want to have to call a woman for permission to deliver. I won, of course.

I loved my job, but my husband said it was the worst thing that ever happened, because after that I had too many opinions and opened

Elizabeth at the Latin Quarter Club, 1952

my mouth too much. My advice? You have to keep an open mind and keep your hopes alive. Hope for the best!

The young people have to keep their ideals in their mind and work toward them for the next elections. It's not going to change overnight for us now. I do think women should work, because it makes us independent, and perhaps their work is more appreciated at work than at home.

Elizabeth at age 86 (photo by Mary M., Los Angeles)

Advice for the country at this moment
I feel very bad for young people who have to work so much and can't get ahead. But if you want things to change, you have to get out and start working on it right now. Find people to join who have the same goals.

It is important for the future how we raise our children. I enjoyed my children. I let them experiment—our living room was a blanket fortress for a long time. I brought shopping bags full of books from the library to read to my children. My daughter wanted to have her own library card when she was three, but she had to learn to sign her name first, so she did.

I wanted them to see all the historic events in New York, so we went to see John F. Kennedy, a ticker-tape parade for the first astronauts, and, of course, the Thanksgiving Day parades.

On vacations we went to a working farm and to see national parks and a lighthouse. We did all this on no money at all. I was very strict with the family budget, so we would have a little money for experiences.

And I became a Girl Scout leader, which set a good example for my daughter, who became a lawyer. I also went to hundreds of basketball games to root for my son and drove him to a music school every week. It's a mother's job to help her children form themselves.

Later on, when we had a chance to travel, we always did crazy things, like explore the sewers of Paris and have picnics on the roadside in Italy with carrot-throwing contests. In my 80s, I tripped and knocked out my front teeth, and with the settlement, instead of buying all new teeth, we took my wheelchair on Alaska and Baltic cruises (to Russia! I saw the Hermitage!) and a tour all over Spain. I say experiment with new things. Yesterday, I tried a persimmon!

"If you want things to change, get out and start working on it right now."

"I got through it all with support from my family and friends and a strong faith in God."

MARGARET ELIZABETH SCHNEIDER, 104
York, Pennsylvania

- Born April 1912 in Violet Hill, Pennsylvania
- Homemaker who tended large vegetable and flower gardens
- Mowed her own lawn until age 96
- Lived alone after her husband died in 1980 until she broke her hip in 2011
- Says keys to living longer than 100 years are: believing in God, loving everyone (no exceptions), helping others, keeping busy, and forgiving
- 3 children, 7 grandchildren, 6 great-grandchildren

Margaret, age 6 and age 18

How I have overcome personal setbacks

When I was ten years old, my father was put in prison, and we went bankrupt. We traveled all over the country looking to make a fresh start. We even had to live in a tent in Florida once!

Margaret when she was dating her future husband

After my dad died young, I had to quit school in sixth grade and go to work in a sewing factory. Then my youngest sister was accidentally shot and killed. I got through it all with support from my family and friends and a strong faith in God.

The best advice I ever got about recovering from difficult times

My mother always told me to not dwell on my problems by looking back at the past. She taught me to keep praying for better days ahead, work hard, and help others in worse shape than me.

How the country recovered from challenging times

I was married during the Great Depression, and those were very hard times with little money. My husband had trouble finding a job, and when he did, the pay was poor. We made extra cash by weaving rag rugs and selling them for a few dollars. When my first child was born, he needed emergency surgery, and I got sick as well. We had no health insurance, so our family chipped in to pay the medical bills, which we gradually paid back. Later I nearly died with typhoid fever. We did what we could to survive, and with God's help, we made it!

When the country was at its best

I liked the Roaring '20s, when I danced the Lindy: "Look for the Silver Lining"!

My experiences with sexism and advice to young women

I was sexually molested by a relative, but I never told anyone. I just forgave him and tried to forget about it. We can't change the past, so what good would it have done if I'd kept thinking about it?

Advice for the country at this moment

Work hard to help yourself, and don't dwell in the past. Love everybody and forgive anyone who hurts you. Try to do the best you can wherever you are to help others. Always pray for better days ahead, and share your blessings with others who aren't as fortunate.

"Roosevelt's fireside chats were soothing and helpful. The entire nation sat still to listen and feel comforted."

ESTELLE LIEBOW SCHULTZ, 98
Rockville, Maryland

- Born June 1918 in New York City
- 2 children, 3 grandchildren, 4 great-grandchildren
- Retired educator, former assistant superintendent of the Compton Unified School District in California

The best advice I ever got about recovering from difficult times

When my husband, Henry Schultz, died 12 years ago, I cried and I cried and I cried. The advice I received was, "Don't worry about crying, but go on with your life." That advice came from me. I made that up.

The Liebow Family in 1934: Bessie, Irving, Ruth, Ely, Estelle, and Naomi

How the country recovered from challenging times

We just muddled through during World War II. President Franklin Delano Roosevelt was marvelous at that time. His fireside chats were incredibly soothing and helpful then. The entire nation sat still to listen and feel comforted.

My experiences with sexism and advice to young women

I really never experienced sexism as such. I did my job, I knew my job, and I was fair, and I listened. Men treated me as their equal. My advice is: learn your job and do it well. Do it better than anyone else.

Advice for the country at this moment

This is a democracy. Keep an open mind, and carry on.

Estelle (top) in a war plant during World War II, 1942; working her way up to be assistant superintendent in the Compton, California, school district, early 1970s; Estelle and Henry Schultz (right) at their 50th anniversary party, 1991

BETTY PRINTZ SIMS, 97
Bethesda, Maryland

- Graduated from Grinnell College
- Joined the U.S. Marine Corps
- Worked as a stewardess
- Had a career teaching music
- Since retirement, has continued to volunteer through music
- 2 daughters, 6 grandchildren, 6 great-grandchildren, 1 great-great-grandchild

How I have overcome personal setbacks

My father died in 1937. It was my last year in high school. My mother and my sister and I were all in shock. He had pneumonia and had an oxygen tent over him for three days, and then he died. I just went on living: I had to continue my schooling and assume a normal life. You don't just sit back and moan and groan; you have to carry on. Don't give in or give up.

How the country recovered from challenging times

When World War II broke out, we had no idea what was going to happen. I was teaching school in Iowa and felt I could not continue teaching with the country at war, so I quit. I joined the Marine Corps, choosing the Marines because I had an ancestor who had been in the Colonial Marines. I expressed interest in aviation, and I was placed in Fixed Gunnery, a training set-up for pilots to learn how to shoot while they fly.

The spirit of the American people working together is what gave us resilience and led us toward recovery, with the assistance of other countries with whom we were fighting. We had food rationing, tires had to be retreaded, cigarettes rationed along with materials needed for the war, like aluminum. It was common to have a victory garden. There was a sense that we all had one purpose. People's attitude was cheerful because they had utter faith in our country.

When the country was at its best

Our country was at its best both during World War II and when John F. Kennedy was president.

"The spirit of the American people working together is what gave us resilience and led us toward recovery."

Betty (left) in high school, Sac City, Iowa; as a U.S. Marine in World War II

He had youth and vigor and sincerity, and he made us feel united. "Ask not what your country can do for you. Ask what you can do for your country" meant that we should continue helping and doing for our country. He renewed our enthusiasm and made us feel proud to be American.

My experiences with sexism and advice to young women

In World War II, the male Marines did not want the women Marines. They called us names, and there was a lack of respect in certain situations.

I experienced no trouble in my job, but others did. They thought that women couldn't do the jobs—not smart or efficient enough. Six thousand women replaced six thousand men so they could go off to war. I think we just worked hard to disregard men's attitude and get the job done.

Advice for the country at this moment

People who believe in our country should stick together, hang on, and work together. Find people who agree with you and work toward things you think are important that the Administration might be ignoring. Don't give up.

"Don't make things worse by causing trouble, but let your voice be heard."

STELLAJOE ENGLISH STAEBLER, 100
Centralia, Washington

- Born June 1916 in Knoxville, Tennessee
- Worked as a secretary, including civil service jobs during World War II
- Peace activist and conservationist, among other volunteer roles
- Was married for 51 years
- 3 daughters, 4 grandchildren, 4 great-grandchildren

How I have overcome personal setbacks
I always made an effort to think positively when things were disappointing. I can accept that and know that there was an alternative. For instance, I always said if I wasn't meant to be a missionary, go to China, and be a teacher, I had another hope that I would find a man I wanted to marry and have some children and raise them the right way, and maybe they would in turn work for other people. And that's all come true, which increases my positive thinking.

The best advice I ever got about recovering from difficult times
My dad said, "You can't bear the whole world on your shoulders." But my mother always had faith and trust in me, and in her other children too, that they would do the right thing. She never doubted that, so she didn't give advice, because she didn't think we needed it. Nobody ever gave her advice when she was growing up.

When the country was at its best
I was proud to be an American during World War II. Until we dropped the atomic bomb; then I was ashamed. I was glad it stopped the war, for the time being. But what a price!

Stellajoe as a young woman

I thought the country was better for a time after Japan surrendered, but that didn't last long; all the wars in the east.

I felt good when Obama was elected. I think that was a hopeful sign. But now I think our country is at a low point.

My experiences with sexism and advice to young women

I was told I couldn't be an accountant. That's what I had decided, to go through high school and take a commercial course to be a CPA. But my teacher told me Tennessee didn't certify females. That felt kind of backward. I probably could have gone to another state, but not Tennessee. One certainly couldn't be female and be president.

Advice for the country at this moment

I would tell a young person who is disillusioned to let your voice be heard when it's needed. Don't make things worse by causing trouble, but let your voice be heard. I think they should challenge the results of the election, and maybe change the system of electoral votes. I think it's maybe archaic.

LOIS EDNA ROTH GARMHAUSEN STEARNS, 100
Burlington, North Carolina

- Born July 1916 in Ashland, Pennsylvania
- Taught school until she retired
- Met Eleanor Roosevelt twice
- Proudly received 100th birthday letter from President Obama
- At 81, eloped from retirement home to marry 76-year-old second husband
- 2 children (from earlier marriage)

Lois (left) at age 3 (photo by her father); in 1926 at age 10

How I have overcome personal setbacks

The Depression was very difficult. I remember the day that the banks closed. I literally had 15 cents in my purse, and my parents didn't have much more in their pockets. I still treasure nice soap as a present because things like soap and toothpaste were so hard to come by during the Depression.

My family and I were able to get through the Depression with hard work and much focus, but organizations such as the WPA and Reconstruction Finance Corporation (RFC) were critical for helping us move forward. Stronger together.

The best advice I ever got about recovering from difficult times

My father was a central and guiding force in my life. He always treated me as an equal, albeit a bit younger than him. He was a coal-mining engineer, with an office in the state capitol building in Charleston, West Virginia. He took me to Washington, DC, when he was on the National Bituminous Coal Commission. He'd also take me into the mines, even though most

"My mom bought me boys' overalls when she realized I was going to hang upside down in trees no matter what."

117

Lois during the Depression

young women did not go down there.

My mother was a strong woman and also a guiding force, but she had a more traditional role. She did buy me boys' overalls when she realized I was going to hang upside down in trees after school no matter what (so a dress wouldn't do).

How the country recovered from challenging times

Personally, the WPA had an important influence on my life. In 1933, the WPA provided my first job after high school when I was 16 years old. They paid one dollar a day for everyone who worked for them. I worked as a counselor at a camp for underprivileged children, and in addition to the dollar a day, I got transportation and meals at the camp. We spent two weeks on the Ohio River and two weeks in the mountains. At the end of the camp, I had saved 30 dollars. I had never seen that much money in my life. I felt like I was rich.

My experiences with sexism and advice to young women

I can't really remember experiencing sexism. I didn't have the time or patience for it. I started driving when I was 14 years old. In 1938 I drove across the country to Montana with my mother. It was a fun trip—it didn't occur to me not to do things like that just because I was a woman. And I sure wasn't going to let anyone stop me.

When I started teaching at Fairview High School after college, I absolutely did not get along with the principal. I went home and cried every day after work. I told my father that I wanted to quit, and he said, "I'll support you until you find another job, but I want to tell you that wherever you go in life, you'll run into someone who is hard to get along with. So you're going to figure out how to deal with that."

Based on these words, I decided to stick it out. And, lo and behold, the principal quit after a few months, and I got along just fine with Mr. Malcolm, the principal after him. I stayed in that job for five years, and I learned that hanging in there and keeping the focus on what you need to do is the best way to go.

"It's very important to keep a sense of humor. It helps no matter how bad things get."

FLORENCE TAUB STEIN, 100
East Windsor, New Jersey

- Born November 1916 in Brooklyn, New York
- Graduated from New York University and earned a master's in social work from Columbia University in the first year the degree was offered
- Had a successful career as medical social worker, retiring as director of social work at St. Luke's-Roosevelt Hospital, Roosevelt Division
- Served on the boards of Jewish Family Services and Cancer Care
- Enjoys playing bridge and canasta at continuing-care facility
- 2 children, 2 granddaughters

Florence as a young woman

How I have overcome personal setbacks
It was very sad for me when my mother died suddenly of a heart attack when I was with her. I coped by taking care of whatever I had to deal with and reaching out to my siblings to deal with it together.

Florence with a deer at Catskill Game Farm

The best advice I ever got about recovering from difficult times

My parents modeled the importance of being charitable. My mother gave to every single charity who requested help. It showed me the importance of giving back to the world and focusing on helping others instead of focusing on my own problems.

How the country recovered from challenging times

World War II was a very stressful time. We just lived one day at a time. I thought Hoover was a terrible president and convinced my parents, who had always been Republicans, not to vote for him again, but to vote for FDR.

When the country was at its best

I think things were good after Johnson, because he did a lot for civil rights.

My experiences with sexism and advice to young women

I was fortunate to be in a mostly female-led field, social work, so I wasn't too affected by sexism. When men eventually joined the field, they were often given leadership positions over women. This was upsetting to me. I was in a leadership position myself by that time, so it didn't affect me personally. I think young women have to join together to fight for what's right.

Advice for the country at this moment

I hope young people will come together and be activists to resist Trump and watch out that he doesn't get away with things. I also think it's very important for people to keep a sense of humor. It helps no matter how bad things get.

"There are a lot of women leaders now. There's nothing stopping them now."

ROSE STOLLER, 98
Chicago, Illinois

- Born June 1918 in Milwaukee, Wisconsin
- Has been an avid, lifelong volunteer and finds elections particularly meaningful
- Volunteered as an election judge for 50 years
- 3 children, 6 grandchildren

Rose (left) in the 1940s and at her 1946 wedding

How I have overcome personal setbacks

I always said that my life began when I got married. I had a good marriage; I was happy. My husband was on dialysis for three and a half years. Twice a week he used to go. I hugged him when he was dying. I kept saying, "I love you. I love you." I don't think he heard me. But I felt good saying it.

After a tragedy, you have no other resources except to put your chin up and go on, day to day. Every day can be better.

The best advice I ever got about recovering from difficult times

You just have to bide your time. There's nothing you can really do except keep a good attitude. The hardest thing to do when you've had problems is to keep your attitude up. I can understand why old people get discouraged. But I try not to be discouraged. I think of all the good things I have in my life: my children, my grandchildren especially. I am so lucky. They are so bright and lovable, and they have the freedom to choose what they want to do and in what direction.

How the country recovered from challenging times

This is America. Our attitude in this country has always been promising. It's what has sustained us all of these years. I believe in America and Americans. Not all of them. But most of them are good people with good attitudes. I have faith in the U.S. I'd rather live here than anywhere else.

When the country was at its best

I think when we have had Democratic leadership. I'm not into politics, but I think the Democrats do a better job than the Republicans. Obama's the one I remember the best. He was honorable and just, and I think he will get a good reputation.

My experiences with sexism and advice to young women

I never was really too involved with sexism. I was happy being a woman. I like men. One thing is, there was no one to encourage me to go to college. I wish they had. I took a lot of courses, but I never took them for credit. I went to lectures. Other than that, I'm not well educated.

I've got to give women credit for getting ahead and doing things and leading. There are a lot of women leaders now. There's nothing stopping them now. Look at Hillary. You've got to give her credit. I'm sorry she didn't make it.

My advice to women: assert yourself. Don't be shy. Speak your mind. Be a forerunner. Lead the pack. There's nothing wrong with a woman leader.

Advice for the country at this moment

I was so disappointed with Trump, but after a while I accepted it. It's not the end of the world. I was proudest that all of my granddaughters and my children volunteered for Hillary. We'll live through this. We've all had ups and downs in our life. I don't think I've had too many downs.

We'll survive. It's not the end of the world. I hope Trump's going to make some wise decisions and pick people who make wise decisions. That's all I can do. I don't think the country's going to go down. It's going to stay level. That's the good thing about this country. When someone is bad, there's a way of getting rid of them or shortening their length of stay. I'm glad to be born in this country. There are always bad people, but they're in the minority. I think there are more good people than bad people.

"To young people, I say:
snap out of it. Act, don't mope."

VELVA STONE, 103
Escondido, California

- Born September 1913 in Terre Haute, Indiana
- Spent most of her life in Everett, Washington
- Worked in an insurance office
- Moved with her husband to California after 1974 retirement
- Active in politics and her community
- Progressive and strong supporter of women's rights

How I have overcome personal setbacks

Fortunately, as I look back on 103 years of life, my memories are mostly positive. I choose not to dwell on the past but look to the future. Still, moving from my own home and total independence to an assisted care facility—and nearly total dependence on others—was my most horrendous adjustment. To be helpless, to leave

Velva in high school

my home, dispose of my belongings, and face my closing years in a facility was devastating.

However, I am focusing on the positive blessings of current good health and financial security and the many friends of all ages who visit me on a regular basis. I'm thankful for the genuine, loving attention of my care givers. My mission is to reach out and comfort those who are in far worse situations than I am.

The best advice I ever got about recovering from difficult times

Two books have strongly impacted me and guided me through difficult times: *Pollyanna* and Joel Goldsmith's *The Infinite Way.*

I was one of eight surviving children. My father was a minister. We supplemented our family diet with produce from the church farm, and my father had a second job in a furniture factory. We were short on everything except love. There was enough of that to go around for all eight of us. Attention and time from my busy father were precious to me.

In second grade I learned about the book *Pollyanna* and excitedly told my father about it. One night after work he presented me a copy. He not only bought the book from scarce funds, he also pledged exclusive time for us to read from the book together every night. Imagine how protected and loved I felt.

People have called *me* Pollyanna because I am viewed as naïve in my optimistic views about the world and situations in my personal life. I am proud to be called Pollyanna. Pollyanna always looked for the positive and the silver lining.

How the country recovered from challenging times

During the Great Depression my seven siblings and their children moved in with Mom and Dad. We pooled our resources and offered mutual encouragement to one another. I walked to work to save bus fare and turned my earnings over to my mother for the common good of our family.

On my long walks to work I saw sad men on corners trying to sell apples for a nickel each. Things seemed hopeless. We had no idea

Velva graduating high school at age 15

124

"In spite of everything, America may be at its greatest today and will be slightly better tomorrow."

Velva and her husband on their wedding day

how long this period of depravation would last. There was no light at the end of the tunnel.

Then came Franklin Roosevelt, the Civilian Conservation Corps, and other New Deal programs. Oh, how we loved him! Oh, how we sobbed to learn of his death in 1945. The key to our recovery was excellent, compassionate leadership. Communities and families pulled together with the realization that we were all in this battle together.

There were acts of kindness. A man brought our family a loaf of bread every morning. Some farmers refused to bid at auctions of fellow farmers' land repossessed by the banks. I believe attitudes toward the poor changed when we saw that poverty was the result of actions beyond our control. The New Deal was the foundation for a stronger middle class.

When the country was at its best

Franklin Roosevelt was a president who gave us hope and progressive policies that built our middle class. As an optimist, I believe in the gradual evolution of a better world. Thus, in spite of everything, America may be at its greatest today and will be slightly better tomorrow.

My experiences with sexism and advice to young women

I was proud to be an expert stenographer, proficient in typing and shorthand. I went to work at 15, after early graduation from high school, and was proud of my accomplishments. The Depression made college out of the question. But later I became an expert on complex insurance issues. When the owner of the insurance agency where I worked died, I was the deserving, logical choice to succeed him. Yet a man without knowledge of insurance was appointed. I trained him to take the position that I had hoped for. Later, I did become an insurance broker, but the path was not easy.

Today sentiment is changing and laws are in place, but there are still battles to be won. Half of our country admires qualities of a man that presents himself as an obnoxious bully. A

125

woman with his attributes would be crucified by the public. How do we turn this around? Forget the men. Educate your children and educate the women who vote for obnoxious candidates opposed to women's rights. As long as women do not support women, we cannot expect real change.

Advice for the country at this moment

To young people, I say: snap out of it. Act, don't mope. Think positive and act positive. Some people believe thoughts are contagious and transmit to other people to form an expanded group consciousness of what is correct. So, think positive, optimistic thoughts and expect progress.

My mother was a suffragette. A month before my seventh birthday the Nineteenth Amendment was passed to award women the right to vote. I was a child, but I was well aware of the time, money, and energy my mother and her associates put into lobbying, rallies, protests, and marches.

You lose your sense of helplessness and feel good about yourself when you make sacrifices and contribute your efforts to support civil rights and other social justice movements.

What has happened to the indignation that drove protests against the Vietnam War? Protests against our participation in the death and destruction in the Middle East are nil. People set themselves on fire to protest Vietnam.

Progressives need a messiah or multiple messiahs to lead rallies, protests, and marches and excite progressives enough to get them out of the house and on the streets. We need people like Bernie Sanders, President Obama, Elizabeth Warren, Hillary and Bill Clinton, and young, positive-thinking women and men to make the American Dream a reality for all the people.

I would love to push my walker into mass protests against the stupid wall and other mindless actions proposed for the next four years. Follow me!

"Look at the bright side of things and know this difficulty will pass."

FRAN TAITELMAN, 99
Eugene, Oregon

- Born March 1917 in Sheboygan, Wisconsin
- Lived most of her life in Wisconsin
- Worked as a bookkeeper
- Was married for 65 years
- 2 children, 4 grandchildren, 7 great-grandchildren

How I have overcome personal setbacks

My sister was diagnosed with cancer when she was a young woman with two very young children. We were very close, and I was so frightened I would lose her, because a diagnosis of cancer almost always meant death in those days. We kept hope and a very positive attitude that she would survive, and she did!

The best advice I ever got about recovering from difficult times

Look at the bright side of things and remain positive and know this difficulty will pass. My husband was an excellent example of how to live this way. He was always a "glass-half-full" person, and I learned from living with him.

When the country was at its best

After World War II there was much hope and national unity. People could work and buy houses and support their families. It was a very hopeful time.

Fran in her 20s

My experiences with sexism and advice to young women

I went back to work when my children were in junior high and high school, and I really loved to work! I wished I had gone to college and had earned my CPA degree, since I did that type of work and was good at it. I encouraged my daughters and granddaughters to get an education and a profession. Now I want to tell my great-granddaughters too.

Advice for the country at this moment

I am so glad I got to vote for a woman for president in my lifetime. I loved it! But Trump is the president-elect, and we have to cope with it.

VIRGINIA FORWOOD PATE WETTER, 97

Havre de Grace, Maryland

- Born August 1919 in Havre de Grace, Maryland
- When first husband died at 44, took over his radio business
- In 1960s was chairman and CEO of the Chesapeake Broadcasting Corporation, one of five female broadcast managers in the U.S.
- Won several lifetime achievement awards, including the American Broadcast Pioneer Award of the Broadcasters Association of America and an honorary doctorate from the College of William & Mary
- 3 children, 6 grandchildren, 9 great-grandchildren

How I have overcome personal setbacks

In 1958 my son had a bike accident and was thrown in the air only to land on his head. He was unconscious for over three weeks. It was a scary time. Then only two years later my husband died suddenly of a massive cerebral hemorrhage at age 44. I was left with three children, a mortgage, and a business. The latter was a blessing, and I went to work the day after his funeral. How do we survive these things? I think we do it by keeping on, moving ahead, having faith in God, prayer, and "true grit."

How the country recovered from challenging times

The McCarthy era was particularly difficult. He accused so many people falsely, and I knew some of them. We had a friend who taught Russian at

"There will be a competent woman president soon. I may not live to see it, but I am confident that it will happen."

a large university, and he was singled out and accused of anti-American activity, because he had gone to Russia to study. It was terrible the trouble McCarthy caused innocent people, and the Senate went along with it blindly. Senator Millard E. Tydings, Maryland, was one who fought McCarthy tooth and nail. He was a personal friend of my family. However, McCarthy had gained so much influence that he was able to influence the next election and get Tydings defeated in that senatorial election. Finally, the tide turned, and McCarthy was recognized as the fraud that he was.

When the country was at its best
In my lifetime, this country was at its best during World War II. There was a true community spirit, and everyone worked together for one cause. We endured food stamps, fuel rationing, food rationing, etc., with little complaint.

My experiences with sexism and advice to young women
I feel quite lucky where sexism is concerned. I simply have not experienced the rejection and/or difficulty others have. When I assumed my deceased husband's position, everyone came to my help. I have no recollection of feeling put upon because I was a female. My late husband's colleagues went out of their way to help me, and I was grateful.

Advice for the country at this moment
I was not only disappointed when Hillary Clinton did not win, but simply appalled that Donald Trump got the electoral vote. I was in a state of shock for days. But I have always had

Virginia at age 19, 1938

a philosophy of "this, too, will pass," and found that most often things are never quite as bad as anticipated.

I also think the time has come to abolish the Electoral College and go to the popular vote to determine the outcome of elections. The electoral vote is out of date now.

Right now, I feel we need to take a wait-and-see attitude. Mr. Trump will either succeed or fall flat on his face all on his own. So we have to let him do that. For the sake of our country, I hope one or the other happens quickly. As for Hillary, my heart aches for her, but I think it has saved her life. I have been terrified that some crazy would take a shot at her. She still is the first woman nominated by a major party to run for the presidency. Also, I would hope the press learned a lesson and will now report facts instead of speculation and also not rely on these endless polls, which turned out to be all wrong! We are on the way, and there will be a competent woman president soon. I may not live to see it, but I am confident that it will happen!

"My advice is that everyone should be an intelligent voter."

ALICE MARIE JOHNSON WHITLEY, 96
Lake Tapps, Washington

- Born November 1919 in Kent, Washington
- Graduated University of Washington with nursing degree in 1943
- After raising children, worked for Conference Committee into her 90s
- Proud and active League of Women Voters member for nearly 50 years
- 5 daughters, 11 grandchildren, 14 great-grandchildren

How I have overcome personal setbacks
I always plan that everything will turn out for the best. I try not to think about the sad things that happen to me. If things don't go the way I want, I just say, "I'm not going to think about it."

How the country recovered from challenging times
During World War II. That was so scary. I wasn't always sure which side was winning or losing. I didn't know what would happen in our future. When the troops came back, they were offered free education. My best friend from University of Washington nursing school was Betty, and she was in the Army Nurse Corps. When she got back, she took advantage of the free education offered. She got a doctorate and did the first sleep study in the United States. Now there are sleep labs all over the nation, and everyone knows about sleep.

When the country was at its best
When the troops came home and everyone was offered a free education. It changed our nation when they had more education. Because people ended up with doctorate degrees and had done all this research.

And with Obama as president and his wonderful Affordable Care Act. He goes down as one of the very best.

My experiences with sexism and advice to young women

It has gotten easier being a woman in our country, because we have equal rights and are accepted with men. I believe the U.S. will elect a female president soon. Women have come a long way in everything else. When I had my children, all the women were staying home, and I didn't have any friends that had a job. Look how much it's changed in two generations. It will gradually change more.

Advice for the country at this moment

My advice is that everyone should be an intelligent voter. They can get information from the League of Women Voters. I appreciate the League of Women Voters, because when they take up an issue, they study it for three or four months, and they always have someone that has a different position on issues than the others in the group. So you hear both sides of the issue. I have been involved with the League since the '60s.

Thirty or forty years ago, I did a prison study and thought that was fascinating. There were 1300 prisoners in Tacoma waiting to be deported, because they'd come in illegally and committed other crimes. I was concerned because it cost 30–40 thousand dollars a year to keep them in prison. It was a very expensive program. I was impressed to learn about this, because I had no idea it was costing our government that much money to take care of our prisoners.

Alice as a child in the 1920s and as a young woman

Editors' note: Alice Whitley passed away in December 2016. Her granddaughter told us that at the funeral, the pastor mentioned how excited Alice was about this project the day before her death. "I know my grandma would just be giggling to know that it will actually be published!"

A Political Scientist Reflects
on a Century of Women's Evolving Roles

BY MICHELE L. SWERS

Professor of American Government, Georgetown University

In 2020, the country will celebrate the 100th anniversary of women's suffrage. The women who share their stories in this volume embody and have borne witness to the epic historical events that have shaped American history since women won the right to vote—from the Great Depression and World War II to the social and political upheaval surrounding the movements for civil rights, women's rights, and the Vietnam War. Living through this history, they experienced the evolution of women's place in American society.

As members of the Greatest Generation whose formative years were shaped by the Great Depression and World War II, these women express tremendous faith in the institutions of American government and exhibit a strong communal and civic spirit. The Great Depression had a devastating impact on many of their families. They recount the loss of homes and family businesses, the closing of banks, and widespread hunger and deprivation.

Yet these challenges also cultivated a civic spirit in society. Velva Stone, 103, recounts that "communities and families pulled together with the realization that we were all in this battle together." Stone walked to work to save bus fare and gave her earnings to her mother "for the common good of our family." She also describes acts of kindness: "a man brought our family a loaf of bread every morning" and "some farmers refused to bid at auctions of fellow farmers' land repossessed by the banks."

The women also point to Franklin Delano Roosevelt and his New Deal programs as saving the country and giving them faith in presidential leadership and government efforts to improve the economy. Many of the women credit the Works Progress Administration, the Civilian Conservation Corps, and the National Youth Administration with providing jobs, supporting the arts, and building infrastructure.

World War II cemented their sense of patriotism and belief in sacrificing for the common good. As 101-year-old Julia Cook puts it, "People worked with a purpose to support our troops." Says Dorothy Barton, 98, "We tightened our belts and became creative and determined in overcoming adversity. We conserved and felt strong, knowing that our sacrifices were necessary for our freedom."

They had husbands, brothers, and sometimes sisters serving in the war. Some lost loved ones in battle. Faye Butler describes the pain of receiving "the terrible telegram" informing her parents that her brother was killed while serving in "Merrill's Marauders in Burma." She also recounts the joy of V-J day, when she celebrated in the streets with her husband Bob, who was on a leave and slated to be redeployed before victory was declared.

The temporary wartime change in women's roles helped sow the seeds for the feminist movement's re-emergence and, later, demands for equality in the workforce. With so many men deployed overseas, many women stepped out of their homes and began working in factories. As Rose Kaufman, 102, puts it, "Women went to work in men's jobs. Rosie the Riveter was praised."

The women in this volume took a range of jobs during the war. Betty Printz Sims quit her teaching position and joined the Marine Corps, working in "Fixed Gunnery, a training set-up for pilots to learn how to shoot while they fly." Twin sisters Mae Belle Powell and Mary Belle Roach worked on bomber planes and built Jeep carburetors. Harriet Terry Robinson Cohen left home for the first time, traveling by train across the United States and by ship from San Francisco to join the Red Cross on the Pacific island of Saipan.

After the war, Rosie the Riveter and her compatriots went home. The economy was booming, returning soldiers went to college on the GI Bill, and the country experienced a baby boom. Cornelia "Neal" Coxe Brewster recalls: "We were all building houses and having babies." Many married women in the suburbs became restless for more intellectual stimulation and responded to Betty Friedan's *Feminine Mystique*, which argued that women

should be able to combine career and family. Other women—including minority women, widows, and the poor—worked out of necessity, though discriminatory labor practices meant they often earned less than men.

The Bureau of Labor Statistics reports that between 1948 and 1975 the percentage of U.S. women who were in the workforce climbed from about 33 to 46 percent. But societal attitudes about women's roles limited their options. Juliet Relis Bernstein, 103, says, "Girls were limited in the kind of career they could pursue—teaching, nursing, secretarial work, or marriage." Indeed, many of these women worked in those fields or assisted in their husbands' businesses. Women of their generation were not expected to go to college.

Those who did try to pursue higher education faced discrimination. Katherine Blood Hoffman was accepted to Duke's medical school, but she refused to "sign a waiver promising not to marry while in their medical school… because Duke didn't require the same promise from men." Indeed, without protections that would later become law, working women who became pregnant were expected to quit—or be fired. Beatrice Lumpkin reports that in 1949 she "was fired from two jobs for being pregnant. As late as 1964 my boss told me, 'For what I'm paying you, I could get a man.' Then he fired me and gave my job to a man I had trained!"

Many women experienced pay discrimination because it was assumed that men were the family breadwinners and therefore needed to be paid more. Dorothy Fischer did not complain when she was paid less, because "that's the way it was and I didn't want to get fired." Inez Alcorn recounts how in "1956 as a checker in a large chain grocery store, I was paid 15 cents an hour less than a 16-year-old box boy. I made 85 cents, and he made a dollar."

The feminist and civil rights movements of the 1960s and 1970s chipped away at these discriminatory practices through legislation prohibiting unequal treatment, including the Equal Pay Act of 1963, the Civil Rights Act of 1964, and the Pregnancy Non-Discrimination Act of 1978. Later came 1993's Family and Medical Leave Act and, in 2009, the Lilly Ledbetter Fair Pay Act. Women brought complaints to the Equal Employment Opportunity Commission and engaged in litigation to ensure enforcement of civil rights laws.

As views on women's place in American society continued to evolve, these women encouraged their daughters and granddaughters to get a good education in order to pursue their dreams. Throughout their lives, they also continued to engage in community building by volunteering for churches and a plethora of civic organizations. Vernice Warfield, 101, became a Methodist minister and pioneered integrated PTAs in her city, working as a civil rights leader and community organizer for the Urban League, NAACP, Church Women United, and Red Cross. Many of the women worked with the PTA, League of Women Voters, labor organizations, hospital auxiliaries, religious charities, peace groups, and the Democratic Party.

To be sure, their educational and career opportunities were limited by their times. But when these women cast their ballots for the first female major party nominee, they were voting for a woman who was a product of the greatest achievements of the women's movement, a prominent lawyer who became First Lady, a senator, and secretary of state. As more women follow in Hillary Clinton's footsteps, the daughters and granddaughters of these pioneering women will complete the journey and elect a female president.

Michele L. Swers, who earned her PhD from Harvard University, wrote *Women in the Club: Gender and Policy Making in the Senate* and *The Difference Women Make: The Policy Impact of Women in Congress*. She is coauthor of the textbook *Women and Politics: Paths to Power and Political Influence*.

ACKNOWLEDGEMENTS

So many people helped to make this book a reality. Neither the book nor the website would have been possible without Roberta Schultz Benor. She put in countless hours communicating with participants and the media, and she contributed her excellent editing skills and smart suggestions. Her input shines through on every page. Thanks also to Shawn Fields-Meyer, who contributed her design expertise and advice on all levels. Special thanks to Carolyn Starman Hessel, Dina Hellerstein, Aaron Hornkohl, Tara Rae Miner, Patricia Marshall, Claire Flint Last, and Luminare Press. We would also like to thank Miriam Benor, David Benor, Ami Fields-Meyer, Sandey and Del Fields, Lora and Jim Meyer, Shep Rosenman, Lois Shenker, Tom Booth, Joseph Gindi, Michael Weiss, Ernesto Yerena, Aliza Benor, Abigail Pogrebin, Rob Kutner, Cathee Weiss, Miriam Heller Stern, Dara Horn, Shawn Landres, Marlene Bane, Shulamith Elster, Rusty Frank, Esther Kustanowitz, Fred Levine, Tricia Thompson, Andrea Michaels, Beth Kissileff, Somchay Edwards, and our many followers and friends on Twitter and Facebook who gave advice and encouragement and helped to spread the word about our project.

We are indebted to Senator Barbara Boxer for a foreword that sets just the right tone and to Professor Michele Swers for taking the time and effort to share her insights and perspective on these women and their times. Thank you to artist Ernesto Yerena for permission to use his image.

We are grateful to the many individuals whose generous donations made this book possible, including: Ezra Benor, Debbie Bunin, Ruth and Alan Bunin, Adele Lander Burke, Lucia Gill Case, Lyn Davis, Elyssa Elbaz, Dan Fields, Nancy Fitton, Rabbi Karen Fox, Caroline Kelly, Fred Kim, Lawrence Kraus, Roselyn Kraus, Beth Marcus, Elaine C. Meyer, Heather Moore, Sharon Morell, Marilyn Rodgers, Michelle Cyr Widolff, and all of the anonymous donors.

Most importantly, we thank the 186 women who submitted their words and photos to the website and the dozens of women who did so for this book, as well as their relatives and friends who helped out.

Finally, special thanks go to our supportive spouses, Shawn Fields-Meyer and Mark Bunin Benor, as well as our children and extended families.

INDEX

ABOUT THE EDITORS

SARAH BUNIN BENOR is an associate professor of Contemporary Jewish Studies at Hebrew Union College. She received her PhD from Stanford University in Linguistics. She is the author of *Becoming Frum: How Newcomers Learn the Language and Culture of Orthodox Judaism* (Rutgers University Press, 2012, winner of the Sami Rohr Choice Award for Jewish Literature) and many articles about Jewish languages and American Jews. She has created several websites, including the Jewish English Lexicon.

TOM FIELDS-MEYER is the author of *Following Ezra: What One Father Learned About Gumby, Otters, Autism, and Love from His Extraordinary Son* and coauthor of *Uniquely Human: A Different Way of Seeing Autism*. Formerly a *People* magazine senior writer, he has written articles for *The New York Times Magazine, The Wall Street Journal*, and many other publications. He assists individuals in writing memoirs and teaches memoir writing in the UCLA Extension Writers' Program.

For more information or to order copies of this book, visit
WWW.WeTheResilientBook.com.